WHAT KEEPS YOU FROM BEING ALL THAT GOD HAS CALLED YOU TO BE?

Whatever it is, you need to know this: there is a better way. God wants you to face your fears and lean-in to who He desires you to be. If you're ready, Facing Your Fears is a great place to start.

Facing Your Fears, a 40-day, Scripture-driven devotional by Bethany Barr Phillips, helps reveal where fear has taken hold of your life and equips you to put an end to these strongholds.

TO VIEW SAMPLES OF FACING YOUR FEARS & TO ORDER, GO TO YM360.COM/FEARS

YOU HAVE AMAZING POTENTIAL TO IMPACT YOUR WORLD FOR CHRIST.

NOT TOMORROW. RIGHT NOW!

Your chance to be used by God isn't just some time in the future. It's now! Your world is rich with opportunities to share the message of the Gospel, and to show people the amazing difference Christ can make in their lives. NOW equips you to make just such a difference.

"NOW" WILL HELP YOU...
- Understand the PURPOSE God has in store for you
- Catch God's VISION for exactly how He wants to use you
- PRACTICE real, practical ways to impact your world
- Commit to ACTING on the opportunities God is giving you

TO VIEW SAMPLES OF NOW & TO ORDER,
GO TO YM360.COM/NOW

THE
RESCUE ✚

interactive
devotional
journal

THE RESCUE interactive devotional journal

© 2016 by youthministry360. All rights reserved.
Published by youthministry360 in the United States of America.

ISBN 13: 9781935832560
ISBN 10: 1935832565

No part of this publication may be reproduced, stored in a retrieval system, or transmitted in any form or by any means electronic or mechanical, including photocopy, audio recording, digital scanning, or any information storage and retrieval system now known or to be invented, without prior permission in writing from the publisher.

Any reference within this piece to Internet addresses of web sites not under the administration of youthministry360 is not to be taken as an endorsement of these web sites by youthministry360; neither does youthministry360 vouch for their content.

Unless otherwise noted, Scripture quotations are from the ESV® Bible (The Holy Bible, English Standard Version®), copyright © 2001 by Crossway, a publishing ministry of Good News Publishers. Used by permission. All rights reserved."

RES
CU
E

interactive
devotional
volume 1

Published by: YM360

TABLE of CONTENTS

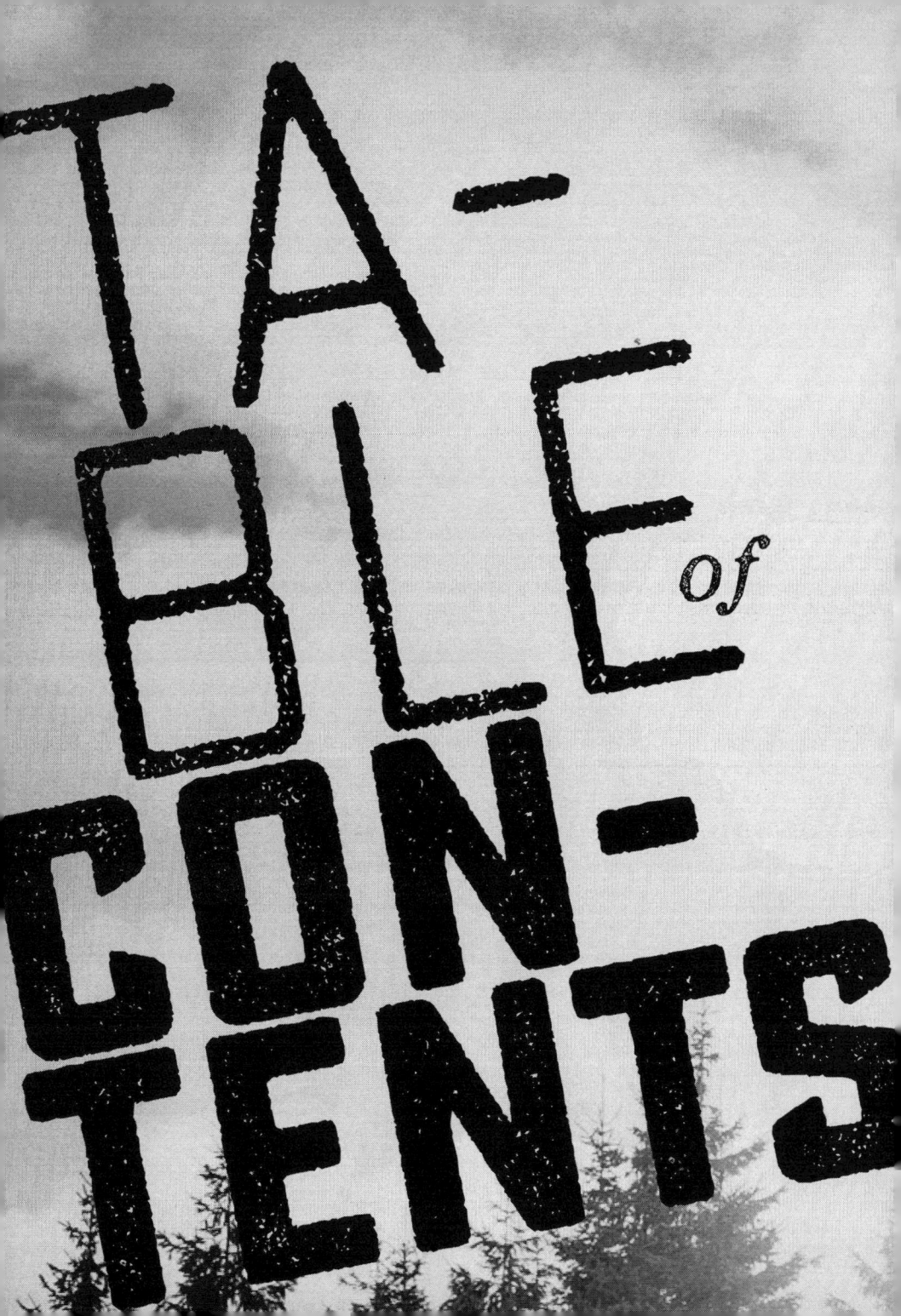

Introduction	1
How To Use This Book	2
Week 1	4
Week 2	8
Week 3	12
Week 4	16
Week 5	20
Week 6	24
Week 7	28
Week 8	32
Week 9	36
Week 10	40
Week 11	44
Week 12	48
Week 13	52
Week 14	56
Week 15	60
Week 16	64
Week 17	68
Week 18	72
Week 19	76
Week 20	80
Week 21	84
Week 22	88
Week 23	92
Week 24	96
Week 25	100
Week 26	104

Week 27	108
Week 28	112
Week 29	116
Week 30	120
Week 31	124
Week 32	128
Week 33	132
Week 34	136
Week 35	140
Week 36	144
Week 37	148
Week 38	152
Week 39	156
Week 40	160
Week 41	164
Week 42	168
Week 43	172
Week 44	176
Week 45	180
Week 46	184
Week 47	188
Week 48	192
Week 49	196
Week 50	200
Week 51	204
Week 52	208
Closing	212
Acknowledgments	213

INTRODUCTION

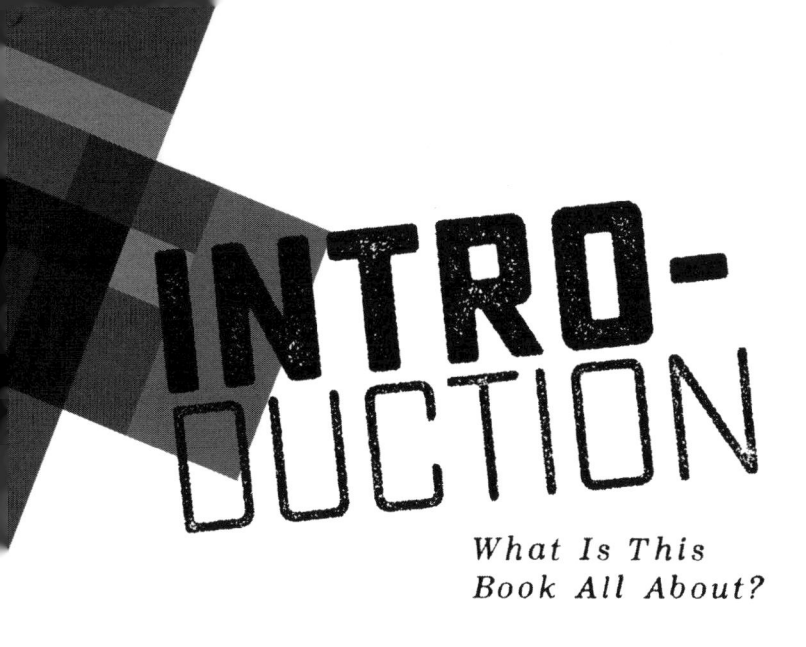

What Is This Book All About?

If you've been around the church very long at all, you've heard the term "the Gospel." You may even know what the word refers to. But do you know how deeply and dramatically the Gospel impacts you and the world around you?

This book is designed to help you grasp this powerful truth.

Put simply, the Gospel is God's amazing Rescue Plan for sinful humanity. Through Jesus, God did what we are incapable of doing: rescuing ourselves from the devastating effects of sin. The good news of the Gospel is that through faith in Christ, we are rescued to a sweeping and far-reaching new reality.

If you're using this book, it's because you're working through The Rescue Bible study in some sort of group . . . a small group, a youth group, or whatever. This book is an interactive devotional companion to the bigger study. The idea behind this book is to help you continue to focus on what you're learning during your group Bible study times. It's an awesome way to fully grasp the power of the Gospel and how it changes you, and the world through you.

God's plan to rescue us from the powers of sin to live a life of freedom and influence is the foundation of what it means to be a Christ-follower. Understanding the Gospel is the key to understanding this. So, get ready to dive in with The Rescue. God's ready to do big things in and through you. What are you waiting for?

HOW DOES THIS BOOK WORK?
for teenagers

3 DAYS A WEEK, 52 WEEKS
If you're holding this book, it means that you're doing a Bible study with a larger group of teenagers entitled The Rescue: Discovering How the Gospel Rescues And Redeems Us. This book is an interactive, companion devotional piece to help you continue to think about the truths you're learning in your group Bible study time.

YOU'LL GET OUT AS MUCH AS YOU PUT IN
You're going to learn a lot in your Bible study time. But that's just a small portion of your week. These devotions keep your heart and mind engaged with God in between your group time. Commit to making time to do these devotions each week. God will honor your faithfulness, and your faith will grow as a result.

HAVE A BIBLE AND A PEN HANDY
Borrow a real Bible, use one Online, or download a Bible app on your phone or tablet . . . whatever you do, it's important that you have one for this journey you're on.

HOW DOES THIS BOOK WORK?
for adults

Teenagers, give us a moment here . . . We need to give some instructions to any adults who may be checking this out.

Adults, for every Rescue Bible study lesson, there are three out of class devotions designed to provide touchpoints for students between your group gatherings. Make sure that you remind students to make time for their devotions during the week. And if you want, shoot them a text during the week to see how things are going.

OK, Teenagers, back to you . . . Turn the page to get started.

the RESCUE

WEEK 1

the RESCUE

WEEK 1
DAY 1

"So I am eager to preach the gospel to you also who are in Rome." – Romans 1:15

Do you want to know a great measure for gauging how you interact with the world around you? Gospel-centeredness. In your family, at school, and doing whatever it is you do for fun, your purpose should be that the Gospel is central in everything. Sounds great, doesn't it? But what does it really mean for us?

Read Romans 1:11-15. Here Paul tells the Roman Christ-followers how much he has "longed" to come visit them. He says, "So I am eager to preach the gospel to you also who are in Rome." Paul is eager to preach the Gospel to the Romans. But wait! They're already Christ-followers, right? So why would Paul be so eager to preach the Gospel to people who already know it? Precisely because Paul knows something that we need to know:

The Gospel is not introductory material. It's not basic. You don't graduate from the Gospel. It's not something you move on from.

Many of us see the Gospel as important for being rescued from our sins. But once saved, it's something that can be moved past. Nothing could be further from the truth. The Gospel has to be at the center of your everyday life. So how does this concept impact what you do as a teenager living in your world?

We could answer that a LOT of different ways. One place to start is to make sure the concepts of grace and redemption are at work in your interactions with the people you encounter. Another way is to model Christ's sacrificial love. One more? You should always measure culture (music, movies, TV shows, etc.) against the message of the Gospel. Does what you watch or listen to fall in line with the heart of the Gospel?

The Gospel is something you can't ever move on from. Let it saturate your life. It's too important not to.

WEEK 1 DAY 2

Today, and maybe this week, keep a Gospel-journal. A what? That's right, a Gospel journal. You're going to ask yourself the following questions:

- Where did you see the Gospel at work today?
- Where did you encounter something that reminded you of God's grace and love?
- Whom did you meet that really demonstrated the love of Christ to you?
- Whom did you encounter that needs to know Jesus?

In the space provided below, record these thoughts. Do it for a day. Or even two. What you will find is that there are a ton of different moments where the Gospel breaks through into your everyday life. One of the most important things you can do is look for these moments and record them as a way of beginning to look for God moving in your midst.

WEEK 1 DAY 3

Take a moment and read this quote:

"I never see important people—or anyone else—without having the deep realization that I am, first and foremost, an ambassador of the King of kings and Lord of lords. From the moment I enter the room, I am thinking about how I can get the conversation around to the Gospel." - Billy Graham, Just As I Am

Billy Graham is one of the most influential Christ-followers in modern history. God worked through Graham to literally share the Gospel message with millions of people. Graham has been a spiritual advisor to dozens of US Presidents. He's been in the company of foreign dignitaries and business leaders of all types. This makes his words ring even more true, doesn't it?

Here are a few things to consider as you go through your day:
· If Billy Graham had this attitude with some of the most important people in our world, what keeps you from having it with your friends at school?

· What has been your experience with talking about the Gospel to others? How comfortable do you feel doing it?

· Would you say that you have a real desire to see people know Jesus? If your heart isn't broken for those who are separated from God, spend some time in prayer asking God to convict you in this way.

WEEK 2
the RESCUE

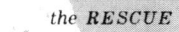

the RESCUE

WEEK 2 DAY 1

"In the beginning God created the heavens and the earth. Now the earth was formless and empty, darkness was over the surface of the deep, and the Spirit of God was hovering over the waters." – Genesis 1:1-2

Think for a minute about your favorite tech gadget. It might be an iPhone, an Xbox, a car, or your favorite set of headphones or ear buds. In order to create that gadget, people researched for years, if not decades, just to develop the technology to make that gadget a reality. Engineers had to figure out how to put all the pieces together so they would work correctly. Designers went through hundreds of ideas to find the right look and feel. Because you use it every day, you probably don't think much about what it took to make that gadget, but it's really an incredible creation.

Read Genesis 1:1-23. Just like you probably don't really think much about what it took to make your smartphone, you might not usually look around outside and consider what it took for God to create our world. God didn't have to do years of research, or try to make a ton of prototypes that didn't quite work before he finally got it right. He just spoke, and our universe came into existence.

Only God could be so powerful to create our universe, the mountains, and the oceans. But our universe isn't just big; it's incredibly detailed, too. Have you ever looked at a plant cell under a microscope? God thought of every detail. And He thought of you, too.

Consider This . . .
· What is the most beautiful place in nature you have ever seen? What does the fact that God created that place say about Him?

· If it's true that God created our universe beautifully and in exact detail, what do you think that means about how He created you?

WEEK 2
DAY 2

If you can, go to a place where you can see something beautiful in nature. It might be a great view of the mountains or just a park down the street.

In the space provided below, write down three things you see that God created. Or, if you enjoy drawing, use the space to sketch what you see on a piece of paper.

1

2

3

Take a minute and pray, thanking God specifically for creating those three things.

WEEK 2 DAY 3

Read this quote and answer the questions that follow:

"A God wise enough to create me and the world I live in is wise enough to watch out for me." – Philip Yancey, *Where is God When it Hurts?*

Consider This . . .
· Have you ever felt like your problems were too small for God to care about?

· Do you agree with Philip Yancey's quote? Why or why not?

· What is one thing going on in your life right now that you really need to know that cares about?

Read the quote again. Then spend some time praying, perhaps saying something like this: "God, you are big enough and wise enough to create our world, so I believe you're big enough and wise enough to care for me."

week 3

the RESCUE

the RESCUE

week 3 day 1

Today's devotion is going to require you to play a little. You're going star gazing. That's right! When was the last time you looked at the sky and thought about the mysteries it contains?

Let's go! If it's night now, go ahead and step outside and look up. You may need to turn off any porch lights or even grab a telescope to get a good view. If it's morning, plan to do this tonight, or check out a cool app like Star Rover HD, Sky View, or Star Tracker Lite. (Free apps like these let you see exactly what the night sky would look like from wherever and whenever you are.) Have fun with it! Do you see any constellations or planets?

Not only are the moon and stars impressive, but also they can be relied upon for navigation, seasons, and calendars. All of God's creation is miraculously purposeful.

Now, grab your Bible and read Psalm 8:3-6.

Looking at space and considering the expanse of God's universe can make us feel pretty small. But consider: in all of creation God desires to have a relationship with you. Just like every star has a place and a purpose, you have a role in His plan. Take some time today to process that and thank God for the plan He has for you in this incredible world!

Consider This . . .
- Write down some of your thoughts as you look at the sky. When you think of your place in God's plan, what are some of the plans you believe He has for your life?

- Here's an idea: why not include members of your family in this activity? Being reminded that God cares about the details might be just what they need to hear today.

the RESCUE

week 3 DAY 2

Read the following quote, and take a minute to think about what it means.
"There are no laws of nature that are self-sustaining. If God were to withdraw for a split second his powerful word, the universe would cease to exist in that same split second. That is why man does not live by bread alone, but by every word that comes from the mouth of the Father." – Graeme Goldsworthy from *According to Plan: The Unfolding Revelation of God in the Bible*

What are your first thoughts about this quote?

Have you ever thought about the fact that the world is spinning and your heart is beating because God is telling it to do so?

The laws of nature (physics, biology, chemistry, mathematics, etc.) are constant because they are part of a purposeful design. God made the world work a certain way, and He is the source of all that is true. You don't tell gravity to work any more than you tell your heart to beat or your body to breathe while you sleep. Think about the significance of that for a minute.

Consider This . . .
- If God has intentionally chosen to give you life for today, what does that say to you about this day having an ordained purpose?

- What do you think God wants to see you accomplish for Him today? Why don't you ask Him?

the RESCUE

week 3 DAY 3

"For we are his workmanship, created in Christ Jesus for good works, which God prepared beforehand, that we should walk in them." – Ephesians 2:10

Have you ever played the game "I Spy"? You know, "I spy with my little eye, something . . . " The trick to that game is the process of elimination. As you ask questions, you narrow down what it's not, and then you can figure out what it is. Sometimes, figuring out God's plan for our life can feel like that.

In this week's lesson we looked at Ephesians 2:10. Our vital role in God's big plan is to do His good works. That's a big concept to define! We cannot understand what it means to be saved for a purpose until we understand what we are saved from.

Read Ephesians 2:1-10 in your Bible.

Paul wrote this to help the church understand the difference between their natural human condition and the new purpose they have in Christ. Relying on our own understanding and desires pleases Satan, not God, and sentences us to a spiritual death.

But look at verse 4 and underline two of the greatest words of all time: **"BUT GOD . . ."** All of the good works that we are to enjoy are gifts from Him. He takes away our death sentence and replaces it with an eternally significant life!

Consider This . . .
· If you were to compare your life before and after your salvation experience, what would it look like?

· What natural tendencies do you have that show the residue of your flesh nature? What desires and abilities do you have that reveal God at work in you?

· If you can't recall your salvation or see no difference in your life, make it a priority to contact a mature believer today to discuss this.

WEEK

FOUR

the RESCUE

WEEK *FOUR* ☐AY 1

"I tell you, this man went down to his house justified, rather than the other. For everyone who exalts himself will be humbled, but the one who humbles himself will be exalted." - Luke 18:14

Have you ever thought about the fact that the spiritual consequence for murder and the spiritual consequence for a white lie is the same? The earthly consequences are wildly different. Murder in the United States is punishable by life in prison or even death in some states, whereas a white lie has no legal ramifications and might even go completely unnoticed by others. But both of these sins are rebellion against God. Romans 6:23 tells us that the wages, or consequence, of sin is death. That consequence is the same for each and every sin.

Read Luke 18:9-14.

Both of these men were sinners. We know this because the Bible teaches in Romans 3:23 that we are all sinners. The difference was that the tax collector knew he was a sinner. He acknowledged his sin and asked God for mercy. The Pharisee wrongly compared himself to other men (feeling very proud of himself) rather than comparing himself to a perfect and holy God (which no one can measure up to). These two men received very different results from their prayers. Look again at verse 14. The tax collector was justified, but the Pharisee was not. Jesus explained that those who humble themselves will be exalted by God.

Consider This . . .
· Do you acknowledge your sin before God and ask for mercy? Or, do you have a tendency to compare yourself to others and feel pretty good about yourself?

· The Pharisee exalted himself because of the "good" things he did, such as fasting and tithing. Do you ever exalt yourself for "good" deeds?

· What do your answers to these questions tell you about your heart?

WEEK FOUR
DAY 2

When we focus on our sins, we may find ourselves feeling guilty or thinking negatively about ourselves. The purpose of repentance is to acknowledge our sins before God so that we may receive forgiveness and meditate on the goodness of God.

Spend some time right now praising God for sending Jesus to save you from your sins. Consider singing a song of worship or, using the space below, writing a poem of thanksgiving. If you have trouble putting this into your own words at first, reflect on Psalm 103 for inspiration.

the RESCUE

WEEK FOUR
DAY 3

It is not uncommon for Christians to feel unworthy of God's love and have difficulty receiving God's forgiveness. We can easily convince ourselves that we're unlovable and become overwhelmed with shame and guilt. The best way to combat these lies is by knowing in our minds and hearts what God says about forgiveness.

Take some time and reflect on the truths of the following verses.

Then, write them down and put them somewhere you can see them when you begin to struggle with feelings of shame and condemnation.

> "IF WE CONFESS OUR SINS, HE IS FAITHFUL AND JUST TO FORGIVE US OUR SINS AND TO CLEANSE US FROM ALL UNRIGHTEOUSNESS."
> **- 1 JOHN 1:9**

> "THERE IS THEREFORE NOW NO CONDEMNATION FOR THOSE WHO ARE IN CHRIST JESUS."
> **- ROMANS 8:1**

> "THEREFORE, SINCE WE HAVE BEEN JUSTIFIED BY FAITH, WE HAVE PEACE WITH GOD THOUGH OUR LORD JESUS CHRIST."
> **- ROMANS 5:1**

5 WEEK
the RESCUE

the **RESCUE**

WEEK 5
DAY 1

"For as by a man came death, by a man has come also the resurrection from the dead. For as in Adam all die, so also in Christ all shall be made alive."
- 1 Corinthians 15:21-22

Death vs. life. There are very few things that contrast as much as that. Have you ever been to the mall and seen a mannequin in a store? It may have on fancy clothes and the coolest styles, but there is clearly something missing. The mannequin may look like a human and dress like a human, yet it is missing the essential quality that it means to be human - life.

Read 1 Corinthians 15:21-12.

Here Paul is introducing two people who are really important to the story of the Bible: Adam and Jesus. They are both guys that made world-changing decisions. Adam chose sin leading to death while Jesus chose obedience leading to life. With a single decision, they each chose to follow different paths - death vs. life.

If we are honest with ourselves, we realize that we are naturally on Adam's path to death. We choose to sin and follow our way over Jesus' way each and every day. If we are going to find true life, we must follow the one whose obedience at the cross leads us to true life. That person is Jesus. He is the only one who can put the broken pieces of our lives and relationships back together. He is the One who can bring the dead to life.

Consider This . . .
· In what ways are you still making sinful decisions that are leading you to walk down a path of death?

· How can you today more fully surrender to Jesus and follow Him in the path of obedience to God which leads to true life?

WEEK 5 DAY 2

Take a moment and read the following quote. Then, think about the questions that follow.

"When we think too lightly of sin, we think too lightly of the Savior." – Charles Spurgeon, *Spurgeon: A Biography*.

What do you think about that quote?

Do you think that's an accurate statement?

Consider This . . .
- Do you take your sin too lightly? Why?

- How does your understanding of sin impact your understanding of God's grace?

- How can you work towards having a healthy understanding of both your sin and God's love for you?

WEEK 5 DAY 3

Today's devotion is going to get you thinking a little bit.

Take some time and think of one or two sins that you really struggle with. Now take a moment and think about how you normally combat that sin. Maybe you've asked someone to hold you accountable or you pray each day that you wouldn't give in to temptation.

Now, let's back up for a minute. Take some time and think about the "why" behind your sin? Are you trying to fit in, gain acceptance, or get control? Are you seeking momentary pleasure or is the sin a result of some insecurity you have? This is a hard exercise and it takes some real soul-searching. If you can't figure out the "why" right now, it's ok. Take some more time and continue to pray and think about it over the coming days.

If you are able to think of the "why" behind this sin, take some time and think about how you're trying to replace Jesus with that sin. That may sound weird, but think about it a bit. If your sin comes from wanting to be accepted, you've essentially rejected the truth that you're accepted in Christ. If you're insecure, you've lost sight of the fact that you're accepted in Christ. If you're seeking momentary pleasure, you're not trusting that Jesus has even greater pleasure intended for you in waiting or abstaining altogether.

This may be new to you and that is totally ok. But when we can start thinking this way about our sin, it helps us get at the root of the problem rather than the symptom. Now, wrap up by taking some time to pray that God would help you truly find what you're seeking in Him, because He's the only place you'll truly find what you're looking for.

WEEK 6
the RESCUE

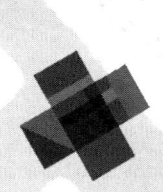

the RESCUE

WEEK 6 DAY 1

"And His name shall be called Wonderful Counselor, Mighty God, Everlasting Father, Prince of Peace." - Isaiah 9:6

Countless superhero movies kill it at the box office each year, and the merchandise flies off the shelves. Why are we so fascinated with super heroes?

Have you ever considered that the reason we are so obsessed with superheroes is because they point us to Jesus and reveal our need for a mighty Savior?

We love that superheroes can do things normal people cannot: super human strength (Jesus is almighty), invincibility (Jesus is indestructible), or incredible speed (Jesus is omnipresent). We cheer on superheroes because they bring justice (Jesus is the righteous Judge) and always come to the rescue (Jesus has rescued us from our sin and an eternity in Hell).

Think about the names of Jesus in Isaiah 9:6. One of those names is Mighty God. Jesus has the ability to do anything. There is no limit to His power.

There are times in our lives when we think something is totally impossible. We look at our situation and think there is no way things are going to be okay. The problem is too big and it seems like there is no way around it. The hurt is way too much, and it doesn't seem like anything can be right again.

Jesus, the one who spoke the world into existence, the one who has calmed the storm, healed the sick, cast out demons and raised the dead, is the Mighty God. Nothing is impossible with Him! He can miraculously make a way for you. He has rescued you from sin and death; surely He can be trusted to rescue you through your problems.

Consider This . . .
· What is going on in your life right now where you need Jesus to be mighty God because there is no other way things are going to work out?

· Do you sometimes doubt God's mighty power? What makes you doubt His ability to do anything He desires to do, even what seems impossible to you?

WEEK 6
DAY 2

How would you describe God's faithfulness to a friend?

First, think about how God has been faithful to you. Then, in the space provided, 3-5 times God has shown His faithfulness in your life.

1

2

3

4

5

Then, write once sentence that describes God's faithfulness in your life. This can be a helpful exercise that will help you articulate this truth to others.

WEEK 6 DAY 3

Using the space below, take some time today and write a prayer to God. Praise Him for being trustworthy and in total control of everything. Tell Him about the times you have messed up and ask for His forgiveness. Thank Him for sending Jesus the Messiah to rescue you from your sin.

week 7

the RESCUE

the RESCUE

week 7 | day 1

"Jesus said to him, 'I am the way, and the truth, and the life. No one comes to the Father except through me.'" - John 14:6

Read John 14:1-6 and pay close attention to verse 6. Jesus said some things to his 12 best friends (the disciples) that can seem confusing. However, when Thomas speaks up to admit he doesn't know what is going on here, Jesus says something very profound: "I am the way, and the truth, and the life. No one comes to the Father except through me."

Did you know that back in biblical times there was a special room in the Temple called "The Holy of Holies" and only priests could enter? This was the place where the presence of God resided. This was how you "got to God." But as we mentioned, only a few could even go to be with Him. Here, Jesus is telling the disciples that the house He has for them won't be like the house of God (Temple) here on earth. It will be one He makes for us. "To get to God" we no longer have to walk through rooms or be special. We just have to believe in who He is and be in a relationship with Him. He is it!!! He is the way back into a relationship with the Lord.

Can you even begin to think about being Thomas, who had never been able to be special enough to go to that part of the Temple to sit face to face with the Lord and to have Jesus tell you that now you can do that freely and it is Him?

Consider This . . .
· What do you think about Jesus being the way, the truth, and the life, and the ONLY way to a relationship with the Lord?

· Think through what that means that God is the way, the truth, and the life. Spend some time writing down each word and brainstorming how that is exactly who Jesus is and why.

the RESCUE

week 7 DAY 2

Look at the three doors pictured below.

On one door, write "Way." On one write "Truth." And on one write "Life."

Now, take a moment and look at these three doors. Go back to the "Way" door and write one thing you know Jesus to be the "way" of for you.

For the door marked "Truth," ask yourself, "how is Jesus the door of truth for you specifically?" Write your answer on the door.

For the door marked "Life," ask yourself, "in what ways is Jesus in your life?" Write your answer on the door.

Don't overthink it. It's OK if you have to think about it for a while. The point is to begin to see how Jesus is that door to a relationship with God.

Then, spend some time in prayer, thanking God for one thing you know to be true about Him today.

the RESCUE

week 7 DAY 3

> "FAITH IN THE LORD JESUS CHRIST IS THE FOUNDATION UPON WHICH SINCERE AND MEANINGFUL REPENTANCE MUST BE BUILT. IF WE TRULY SEEK TO PUT AWAY SIN, WE MUST FIRST LOOK TO HIM WHO IS THE AUTHOR OF OUR SALVATION."
> **- EZRA TAFT BENSON**

Consider This . . .
- As we spend time thinking about Jesus rescuing us from a life apart from Him, what does the quote make you think of?

- Does this quote lead you to talk to God about anything?

Take some time today to let God know how you feel about Him and the salvation He offered to you.

WEEK

EIGHT

the **RESCUE**

WEEK *EIGHT* DAY 1

"And when Jesus entered Peter's house, he saw his mother-in-law lying sick with a fever. He touched her hand, and the fever left her, and she rose and began to serve him." - Matthew 8:14-15

When someone does something nice for you, like give you a gift or pay you a compliment, there's usually some kind of a response on your part. Maybe you thank them through social media or write a thank you card. Sometimes you simply say "thank you." It would be rude not to respond in some way to the kindness of others. But how do we respond to the good things God does for us?

Read Matthew 8:14-17 and note how Peter's mother-in-law responded after Jesus healed her. Matthew records that she got up and started serving Jesus. Think for a second about what this means. The lady was healed and then went back to the normal household duties that women did in Jesus' day. In other words, she responded with action.

So what does that mean for a teenager in the twenty-first century? God loves it when we thank Him for the things He does in our lives. But He also loves it when we respond to Him by ministering to others. Let your thanks to God not only be through words, but also through actions.

Consider This . . .
· Why do you think it is important to respond to God's work in our lives through actions?

· Jesus' miracles and healings pointed people to God and were a preview of God's ultimate act of healing our sins through the cross. Do you think people can be pointed to God's power of redemption through your actions? What is one thing you could do this week to help others see God's love in action?

the RESCUE

WEEK *EIGHT*

DAY 2

"And when it was day, he departed and went into a desolate place. And the people sought him and came to him, and would have kept him from leaving them, but he said to them, 'I must preach the good news of the kingdom of God to the other towns as well; for I was sent for this purpose.'" - Luke 4:42-43

Take a few minutes to think about some times when you have experienced the presence of God in incredible ways. Maybe it was at youth camp, on a mission trip, or during a special church service. In the space below, write down three such experiences.

Now, wouldn't it have been awesome to have just stayed in those moments to keep experiencing God in incredible ways? In the passage you read from Luke chapter 4, Jesus knew the people wanted Him to stay. But He had other places to go and preach. Jesus wants you to have incredible experiences with Him, but He also wants you to come down from the mountain and live out your faith daily.

Thank God for the special moments of His extraordinary presence and power. Ask Him to let you use those experiences to give you the strength to share His love in daily life.

the RESCUE

WEEK EIGHT
DAY 3

Take a moment and read this quote:

"I HAVE NO SPECIAL TALENTS. I AM ONLY PASSIONATELY CURIOUS."
- ALBERT EINSTEIN

Now, that is quite a declaration from what many people say is the most brilliant man who ever lived. That's saying something, isn't it?

Think about this quote and ask yourself the following questions:
- How does passionate curiosity relate to our faith in and relationship to God?

- If you were truly passionately curious about your faith, the Bible, Jesus, etc., how would that change your relationship with God and the way you live out your faith each day?

Let passionate curiosity move you to not only a greater understanding of God, but also to being a better witness for Him.

WEEK 9

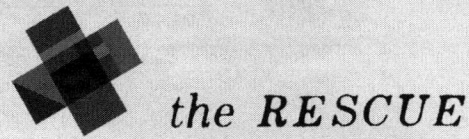

the RESCUE

WEEK 9
DAY 1

"For God did not send his Son into the world to condemn the world, but in order that the world might be saved through him. Whoever believes in him is not condemned, but whoever does not believe is condemned already, because he has not believed in the name of the only Son of God." - John 3:17-18

Did you ever get to ride on a fire truck when you were a little kid? The flashing lights, loud siren, and the unmistakable hugeness of a fire truck make it irresistible to a small child—not to mention the cool plastic helmets you get. Knowing real life heroes and exploring their truck is safe for a child when there is no emergency. But being rescued from a burning building gives a completely different appreciation for that truck!

Read John 3:17-18. These verses, obviously, follow John 3:16—one of the most popular verses that talk of God's love. Verse 16, as well as the passage we are talking about today, was part of a discussion between Jesus and Nicodemus about eternal life. Jesus clearly spoke of God's love and of His desire that the world come to know Him, as He made a way for redemption through Christ. Although God did not send Jesus to condemn or judge the world, judgment will happen, nevertheless. Why? Because of God's never-changing holy character, He cannot allow sin to remain unpunished. Those who reject Jesus will reap the consequences for their sin through eternal judgment; it is their choice. God is love; but, His love is amplified through the judgment required for our sin.

Our culture likes to appreciate the love of God but ignore His holiness and judgment. Overlooking the judgment required of God cheats the message of the gospel—it's kinda like admiring a fire truck for its beauty and functionality but neglecting to see it as a life-saving, heroic tool. If your house is on fire, the fire truck that blasts water to put out the flames suddenly isn't just cool bells and whistles. Your reaction becomes one of awe, humility, and gratefulness.

How does thinking about God's justice bring about a new understanding of the Gospel in your life? Why is the good news of the Gospel most fully "good" when we understand God's judgment?

WEEK 9 DAY 2

Every choice we make is also a rejection of some kind.

Think about it. When you chose to eat cereal this morning, you rejected the oatmeal in the pantry. When you played video games during your free time, you rejected the choice to watch your favorite TV show. When you chose your shirt this morning, you turned down another one.

These are seemingly simple choices with mostly small consequences. But what about those weightier decisions? The choices that we make daily with our time, focus, actions, etc. can hurt or nurture your relationship with God, and, therefore, your proclamation of the gospel.

In the space provided below, write down some of those daily choices that God gives you. Think about (and write) the consequences of how each choice impacts your life.

Write a one-sentence prayer to pray each time you are faced with a choice, asking God for wisdom to make the choice that glorifies Him and the strength to make it.

the **RESCUE**

WEEK 9 DAY 3

"Jesus did not 'model His teaching' like a fashion model parading the latest fad. His lifestyle was not a put-on conceived to strengthen the words He spoke. Jesus simply lived what He taught. What He taught flowed out of Who He was." — Rick Yount

Read that last sentence again.

It can be easy to know all of the right things to say and to live in a way that makes us look pretty good in front of others. But, the authenticity of our relationship with God will always become clear. When it comes to sharing the gospel with our lives and words, our relationship with the Lord flows out of our mouths when it is central to who we are.

Consider This . . .
How does a deeper relationship with Jesus make us more aware of opportunities to share about Him and our faith?

Ask God to deepen your desire to know Him and to make you aware of opportunities to share about Him.

WEEK 10
the RESCUE

the RESCUE

WEEK 10 DAY 1

"For our sake he made him to be sin who knew no sin, so that in him we might become the righteousness of God." - 2 Corinthians 5:21

We've all been a part of a trade. It might have been Little Debbie snacks from our lunch box, Pokémon cards, pencils, or a number of other things back in our elementary school days. Professional athletes get traded all the time. The point of a trade is to win—to get the better end of the deal. If you're able to swap your buddy a Raisin Cream Pie for a Swiss Cake Roll, you win, right? The point of a trade is to get something better in return.

Read 2 Corinthians 5:21.

Wow! This is the worst trade of all time. Jesus takes my sin and, in return, gives me His righteousness. Jesus isn't trading up. He definitely isn't getting the better end of the deal. We sin, but Jesus takes our sin upon Himself and takes the punishment that our sin deserves. Then, in return, Jesus gives us righteousness. In the place of our worst, He gives us His very best.

The unbelievable truth of this verse is that when God sees you, He doesn't see your sins, failures, or shortcomings. Instead, He sees Jesus' perfection, goodness, and love. The worst trade of all time is what rescues us from sin and death.

Consider This . . .
· Why would Jesus make this trade? What does this exchange tell us about the character of Jesus?

· How does it make you feel to know that when God sees you, He sees Jesus in your place? How does it make you feel to know that you can have a relationship with God because of Jesus' trade with you?

· Spend a moment in prayer today thanking Jesus for His willingness to take our sin and give us His righteousness.

WEEK 10 DAY 2

Read this quote and respond to it using the questions below.

"Before we can begin to see the cross as something done for us (leading us to faith and worship), we have to see it as something done by us (leading us to repentance)." – John Stott, *The Cross of Christ*

By us? That can be difficult to consider. Think through these questions as you process what this quote means for your life.

Consider This . . .
- Why do you think it is necessary to first see the cross as "something done by us"? How does this viewpoint lead us to repentance?

- How is the cross something done by you, personally? How does that thought lead you to personal repentance?

- What attitude changes should come from understanding the cross as "something done by us"?

Today, as you think about the truth that it was for our sin that Jesus died on the cross, don't forget the second amazing truth: that Jesus also died on the cross for us.

WEEK 10 DAY 3

We've been exploring some intense topics this week as we've discussed the implications of the cross. Our response to the cross shouldn't only be academic, though.

Spend some time reflecting on some of the amazing truths of the cross.

Then, using the space below, write a prayer to God expressing your gratitude for all that Jesus did for you when He died on the cross.

week 11

the RESCUE

the RESCUE

week 11 day 1

"For by grace you have been saved through faith. And this is not your own doing; it is the gift of God, not a result of works so that no one may boast. For we are his workmanship, created in Christ Jesus for good works, which God prepared beforehand, that we should walk in them." - Ephesians 2:8-10

If you've been at church for any length of time, you've probably heard people talk about grace a lot. It seems to be an important thing to Christians. The idea that the gift that God gives us eternal life is a gift of grace is a pretty big deal. Grace means receiving something great even though you didn't do anything great to earn it. Why is it such a big deal that God's gift of forgiveness and eternal life is a gift of grace?

Read Ephesians 2:8-10.

Look for the answer to the question above in verse 8. Paul says that the reason our salvation was a gift is "so that no one may boast." Isn't that a weird thought? But think about it: if we were somehow able to earn our own salvation, we would be able to look at our lives and say, "Look at what I did!" But here's the cool thing: because we didn't earn it, when we look at how God forgives us, all we can say is "Look what Jesus did!"

Paul ends this part of Ephesians by encouraging us that we are the "workmanship" of God. We are an image to the world of what God can do, and He calls us to walk in the good works that He has created for us to do. This is the cool part of grace. We're not called to work for God to repay Him for His kindness, we're simply responding to what He has given us! Because God has loved us, we obey Him because we love Him too!

Consider This . . .

- Has there ever been a time in your life when you've been more proud of what you've done for God than what He has done for you? Confess that to God and ask Him to build a heart of humility in you. Ask Him to help you glorify Christ with your life!

- What are some of the "good works" that God has called you to "walk in?" Pray that God will give you the strength to walk those out in your life because of what He did for you on the cross.

week 11 DAY 2

Take a moment a think of three things that are different in your life because you know Jesus. Maybe it's the way you treat your family, or certain choices you make, or simply a sense of joy you have because of how He loves you. Write them in the space below.

1.

2.

3.

Now, take a moment to realize that these things are evidence of how God has saved you!

He has made you alive in Christ! In the same way that breathing, walking and smiling can be signs that you're alive, these are signs that you are alive in Christ. Thank God for making you alive in Him and giving you energy to live that out.

the RESCUE

week 11 DAY 3

A lot of times in Scripture, the same guys talk about the same things in different places. We've been talking about how Paul describes our salvation in Ephesians chapter 2. He says a similar thing in Colossians 2:13-14:

> AND YOU, WHO WERE DEAD IN YOUR TRESPASSES AND THE UNCIRCUMCISION OF YOUR FLESH, GOD MADE ALIVE TOGETHER WITH HIM, HAVING FORGIVEN US ALL OUR TRESPASSES, BY CANCELLING THE RECORD OF DEBT THAT STOOD AGAINST US WITH ITS LEGAL DEMANDS. THIS HE SET ASIDE, NAILING IT TO THE CROSS.

Take a minute to think about how you have disobeyed God. It may not be fun, but think about the different ways you have chosen your own way over God's way.

It can be a pretty big list, can't it? Now, take a deep breath. Paul says that Jesus took that list of all the ways we have disobeyed (and even the ways we're going to mess up in the future) and set it aside. He didn't need it. In fact, He nailed it to the cross!

Rest in the fact that Jesus has forgiven you today. Never forget that Jesus actually, really loves you.

WEEK

TWELVE

the RESCUE

WEEK TWELVE DAY 1

Take some time and think about this quote.

"No matter how devastating our struggles, disappointments, and troubles are, they are only temporary. No matter what happens to you, no matter the depth of tragedy or pain you face, no matter how death stalks you and your loved ones, the Resurrection promises you a future of immeasurable good." - Josh McDowell, *Evidence for the Resurrection*

The life of a Christian is not free of struggles. God even promised that in this life we would face tough times (John 16:33).

Consider This . . .
· Do you know that God is for you (Romans 8:31) and is working all things for your good (Romans 8:28)? How does this change the way you see tough times?

· Will you surrender your problems to God and trust that, in His time, He will bring you immeasurable good? What does this look like, practically speaking?

Take some time and talk to God about your struggles. Thank God for the resurrection of Jesus, which brings life and an end to all temporary pain.

the **RESCUE**

WEEK *TWELVE*
DAY 2

"Don't be alarmed," he said. "You are looking for Jesus the Nazarene, who was crucified. He has risen! He is not here. See the place where they laid him." – Mark 16:6

There is power in the resurrection! It changed Mary's circumstances immediately. It changed the course of human history for all eternity! Look through the following Scriptures and think about some of the other instances when Jesus displayed His power.

Matthew 8:24-27 // Matthew 9:32-33 // Matthew 11:4-6 // Luke 5:3-6

Take a second and jot down a few observations from these verses in the space provided below:

This same power, the power that enabled Jesus to perform miracles and rise from the dead, is the same power of the Holy Spirit that now dwells within every believer!

Consider This . . .
· Can you imagine what God can do in your life if you allow His power to work through you?

· Can you envision what God can do in the world if all believers follow the will of God act with His power?

the **RESCUE**

WEEK *TWELVE*
DAY 3

Toby Mac has a song called "Speak Life" released on his Eye on It album in 2012. The premise of the title is how we all have the power to speak life (or death) into someone's life by the things we say and the way in which we speak. Take a second and read these lyrics and pray about some situations the Lord will lead you in where you can "speak life" to someone that is struggling.

> So speak Life, speak Life.
> To the deadest darkest night.
> Speak life, speak Life.
> When the sun won't shine and you don't know why.
> Look into the eyes of the brokenhearted;
> Watch them come alive as soon as you speak hope,
> You speak love, you speak...
> You speak Life, You speak Life.

Now, spend some time writing a prayer to God, asking thanking Him for calling you to be His child. Ask Him to give you the strength to reach out to those in your life who are struggling and need the peace of God. Thank God for the amazing blessings He surrounds you with, even when things don't go as we want them to.

WEEK 13

the RESCUE

the RESCUE

WEEK 13
DAY 1

"[God] has saved us and called us to a holy life—not because of anything we have done but because of his own purpose and grace. This grace was given us in Christ Jesus before the beginning of time, but it has now been revealed through the appearing of our Savior, Christ Jesus, who has destroyed death and has brought life and immortality to light through the gospel." - 2 Timothy 1:9-10

Think for a minute about someone you really admire. It could be an athlete, an author, a teacher, or a parent. What do they do that makes you admire them? Chances are it's something unique or different that other people don't typically do or aren't able to.

Read 2 Timothy 1:9-10.

God's grace that He gives you isn't just about saving you from sin or giving you eternal life. His grace invites you to live with an incredible purpose today. God's grace means that He has called you to a "holy life"—to a life that is different, to a life that chooses every day to respond to God's grace by making a difference in people's lives and loving people in extraordinary ways.

The people you admire choose to live differently. Because of God's grace, you have the opportunity to live differently, to live with a new purpose, to live a life that matters.

Consider This . . .
· What does it mean to you to live life differently—in a positive way—than most people your age?

· Think back to the Bible Study from this week—what was the one thing you chose to do this week from the "Tomorrow" side of the list? How's it going?

the **RESCUE**

WEEK 13 DAY 2

Throughout Scripture we read about how we are "set apart" to live differently than the world around us. Paul refers to it as our "holy calling." In the space provided below, write down a few things that you can do this week to live out your "holy calling."

Now that you've identified these things, there's no excuse not to follow through on them. Decide right now that you're going to take action on the list you made and go out and live a "set apart" life.

the RESCUE

WEEK 13 DAY 3

This week we saw that God gives us His gift of grace simply because He chooses to do so.

Take two minutes to think of and write down as many gifts—good things—as you can that God has given you. Use the space below:

Now, read the list out loud, each time saying, "God, thank you for ____." In the space below, write a short prayer to God, thanking Him for His grace and mercy.

WEEK 14
the RESCUE

the RESCUE

WEEK 14 DAY 1

"Therefore, they are before the throne of God and serve him day and night in his temple; and he who sits on the throne will shelter them with his presence."
- Revelation 7:15

Technology has advanced to the point where we can "be" in many places around the world while sitting on our couches. But, when certain events happen in life, we want to be there in person. Think about it: your graduation, the Super Bowl, your wedding, the birth of a child—these are all things you'd rather experience in person rather than through technology. Some things are just better in person.

Read Revelation 7:15. The literal word used is "tent" or "tabernacle" and is the same idea used when God told Moses to build a tabernacle so that God could live among His people (Ex. 25:8-9). The difference, though, was that His people could not enter into God's presence in the tabernacle. God was with them, but the relationship was strained because of sin. However, we see in Revelation that God's people are with Him—they are in His very presence. The idea of God throwing a tent over His people gives a picture of His shelter and protection, in addition to being with them in a completely restored relationship. Because of Christ's perfect sacrifice, we will be able to stand before God, unafraid and in person.

God is omnipresent, so He is everywhere all the time. We know that in our hearts. But, wouldn't it be cool to actually be in the physical presence of God and without all of the yuckiness of this world to cause problems?! Some things are just better in person. Eternity with our Creator is one of those.

Consider This . . .
· What do you think would be the coolest thing about being in God's presence?

· What sin in your life is causing a strained relationship with God? Confess that to Him now and seek reconciliation.

WEEK 14 DAY 2

What do you think of when you think of the word "filter"? It has become a popular word to use with photographs we take on our phones. On our phones, filters can change colors, highlight faces, or do any number of things. Get out your phone (or your parents' with their permission) and take a picture of something around you that is very ordinary. Then, scroll through the filters for the camera or your social media app. Look at how each filter changes the picture. Which one takes it from ordinary to pretty cool?

Think about filters you have in your life. Everybody has them. These are filters that you use to help you make sense of things going on around you.

Consider This . . .
- What if you had a filter that let you see your circumstances through the truth of eternity? How would that change the way you look at your situations?

- Isn't your faith a filter in some ways? Or better yet, shouldn't it be? List some ways your faith is a filter for how you see the world.

As you go through your week and encounter struggles, pull out your imaginary eternal filter to help give you strength to endure, hope to be joyful, and motivation to overcome.

the **RESCUE**

WEEK 14 DAY 3

In the third book of The Lord of the Rings, Frodo and Sam, two brave Hobbits, find themselves nearly dead after their tumultuous journey to destroy the infamous ring. Upon waking from what he thought was a dream, Sam finds that his dear friend Gandalf is alive. Read the following quote from Sam:

"At last he gasped: 'Gandalf! I thought you were dead! But then I thought I was dead myself. Is everything sad going to come untrue? What's happened to the world?'

'A great Shadow has departed,' said Gandalf, and then he laughed and the sound was like music, or like water in a parched land . . .'" —J.R.R. Tolkien, *The Return of the King*

Imagine if everything sad came untrue. What kind of world would that be?

Jesus and the life He modeled clearly tells us that a life of following Him will be difficult. Bad things will happen. We will hurt and be hurt. Sin abounds in this world; therefore, so does pain and sadness. BUT, God gave us a picture of our future with Him. And in it, all of the sad things come untrue.

Think about Gandalf's statement, "a great Shadow has departed." How are our lives on earth like living under a great shadow, attempting to block all things good?

Of course, the greatest thing about living out from under the shadow is that the saddest thing, being away from God, will become untrue. Try to imagine what that would be like. Write down three words or phrases to describe it.

This week, ask God to give you a true sense of joy and hope that comes with knowing God's ultimate plan for our lives.

week 15

the RESCUE

the RESCUE

week 15 day 1

"And to put on the new self, created after the likeness of God in true righteousness and holiness." - Ephesians 4:24

What if Jesus came to your school today? What if He walked down the halls? Sat in your class? Interacted with your friends in the lunchroom? Wouldn't that be cool? Or would that be scary? Sometimes we think that there are moments in our lives when we would love to have Jesus there, like when we are trying to witness to our friend or when we had the right answer in small group. But there are also moments when we would rather not have Him there, like when we made fun of someone or cheated on a test.

As a Christ-follower, the reality is that you are the representative of Jesus wherever you go. When Jesus left the earth and ascended into heaven, He left us here to represent Him. In Ephesians 4:24, Paul says we are living in the "likeness of God" as new creations. So, if you are a Christ-follower at your school, you are the representative of Jesus walking down the halls, sitting in class, and hanging out in the lunchroom.

When people look at you, do they truly see the likeness of the Jesus we find in the Bible? Are you one who is seeking to live a life like Ephesians 4:24 says that is righteous and holy? To be righteous means to be without blame and to do the right thing, and to be holy means to be set apart as one who follows God. Are those the characteristics that people would use to define you and your life? Is your likeness of Jesus one that points people to Him or away from Him?

Consider This . . .
· How are you going to live differently today realizing that you are Jesus' representative at your school?

· What is one way that you can seek to be righteous and holy in your actions and attitudes today?

week 15 DAY 2

This week in our study we have been talking about growing in Jesus and becoming more like Him. The big theological word for that process is "sanctification." Read the following quote:

"Sanctification means that the Christians have been judged already, and that they are being preserved until the coming of Christ and are ever advancing towards it."- Dietrich Bonhoeffer, *The Cost of Discipleship*

Consider This . . .
- How does the truth that we have already been judged by God help encourage us when we struggle to live the Christian life?

- How does the fact that Jesus is preserving us until He returns encourage us when we struggle to live the Christian life?

- How does the fact that Jesus is growing us to work on His mission until the day that He returns encourage us when we struggle to live the Christian life?

the RESCUE

week 15 DAY 3

In the space provided below, take a few minutes and draw a picture of yourself. That's right, break out your inner-artist and draw yourself from head to toe (no one else has to see this, so your lack of skills is safe).

Then, circle your head, your hands, your feet, and your heart. Draw a line from your head out to the side of the paper and think about what it means that your old self has been put off and you are now a new creation. What does that mean for your mind? What are some ways your mind should function as a new creation? Jot down a few of your answers below:

* Now, do the same for your heart. What impact does being a new creation have on it? How should a new heart function?

· Do the same for your hands and feet. What should you get involved in? Where should being a new creation take you?

· Take a moment and pray over this page. Pray that you would fully embrace what it means to be a new creation in Christ and that every part of your being would live that out.

WEEK SIXTEEN

the RESCUE

the RESCUE

WEEK SIXTEEN DAY 1

"He is the propitiation for our sins, and not for ours only but also for the sins of the whole world." - 1 John 2:2

Have you ever wondered what it would be like to know Jesus? To be around Him? Think about it: He never got mad at something He shouldn't have, He was never selfish, and He never had impure thoughts! He was perfect!

This week we talked about how Christ forgives us. Even though we sin, He makes us blameless. If Jesus forgives us, does that mean we can just sin anyway and everything will be OK? Sometimes it feels that way. It's easy to think that it doesn't matter if we sin because God will forgive us. Read 1 John 2:1-6 and see what John thinks about that.

John was a guy who knew Jesus –he was one of Jesus' best friends. He saw His perfection first hand. John calls us to be like Jesus and to walk in His ways. Because we love Jesus, we follow Him and try to walk as He walked. But, we know we're going to fail at some point.

It's in these moments of failure that John reminds us that we have an advocate who is perfect: Jesus. He says in verse 2 that Jesus is our propitiation, which means that Jesus is the sacrifice that took on the death we deserved. Our sin has already been paid for. When God looks on us, He's not angry with us. He has favor on us! Because God has done that for us, we strive to obey Him—even when it's hard.

Consider This . . .
· Do you ever struggle with not feeling guilty for sinning? Confess that to God and ask Him to always show you your disobedience. Tell Him that you want to live like Christ, and ask for forgiveness for the times you haven't.

· What are some of the commandments of Jesus? What are the hardest ones for you to follow? Pray and ask God to give you the courage to follow Him even when it's hard.

the RESCUE

WEEK SIXTEEN
DAY 2

Look at the two circles below. Take a minute and fill in these circles with how you see yourself and how you think God sees you. Describe yourself and your heart (the good and the bad).

HOW I SEE MYSELF   HOW GOD SEES ME

Now, take a moment to grade yourself. It's simple. If you've placed your faith in Christ, here's the incredible thing: no matter what you wrote in the left circle, the one on the right should read: **"forgiven, blameless, and holy because of Jesus."** Because of the death of Christ, God welcomes us into His family as righteous children!

Thank God for His love as you finish your devotion today.

the RESCUE

WEEK SIXTEEN
DAY 3

What is the biggest sin you struggle with? What is the one thing that you wish you didn't do anymore but always seems to be with you? What causes you to feel guilty?

Remember these two verses from our lesson this week:

"And you, who once were alienated and hostile in mind, doing evil deeds, he has now reconciled in his body of flesh by his death, in order to present you holy and blameless and above reproach before him." - Colossians 1:21-22

Think about that. Jesus presents us **holy and blameless and above reproach** before God!

Even though you struggle with sin, Jesus presents you **holy and blameless and above reproach** before God!

Say that out loud: Jesus presents **ME holy and blameless and above reproach before God!**

Pray and ask God to help you live how He sees you: holy and blameless and above reproach. If you want to write your prayer, use the space below:

WEEK 17

the RESCUE

the RESCUE

WEEK 17
DAY 1

"You are the light of the world. A city set on a hill cannot be hidden." - Matthew 5:14

The Statue of Liberty. Picture it. Lady Liberty towers over Staten Island, New York, welcoming people of all nations to the United States of America. The minute you see her, you cannot help but think of the promise she represents. She is known around the world as a symbol of freedom.

Jesus said that our lives are kind of like the Statue of Liberty. Christians are to stand out and send a message to the world. Read Matthew 5:14.

If Christ has rescued you, the Light of the World lives within you. His light shines through you as you follow Him and seek to bring Him glory in every area of your life. When your heart is fully devoted to Jesus, His light shines through you in the words you use, the things you watch, what you listen to, the activities you participate in, the things that make you laugh, and the people with whom you spend the most time. When someone is in love with Jesus, it is obvious to the world. The light cannot be hidden.

Just as you cannot see the Statue of Liberty without thinking of freedom, the character of Christ should be so obvious in your life that people cannot help but think of Jesus when they see you. Your life is to be a living testimony, communicating the Gospel of Christ to the world.

Consider This . . .
· What are some areas in your life that are not shining with the light of Christ? What choices can you make this week that would help others see the character of Christ in you?

WEEK 17 DAY 2

FIRST, grab a flashlight.

THEN, with all of the lights on, turn on your flashlight. You really don't notice much, do you?

NEXT, turn off all of the lights in the room except for your flashlight. When the lights are out, think about the brightness of your flashlight when the room is already lit and now that the main lights are out.

NOW, turn the lights back on. Did you notice how much brighter the light from your flashlight is when it is surrounded by darkness?

A small light can make a huge difference! Jesus rescued you so that you would be a shining light in a dark world. Following Jesus, even when everyone else around you isn't, makes your light shine even brighter.

The brighter your light shines, the more glory God gets through your life. How will you let your light shine today?

WEEK 17 DAY 3

Take a moment and read this quote:

> "BY DEFINITION, AN INFLUENCE MUST BE DIFFERENT FROM THAT WHICH IT INFLUENCES, AND CHRISTIANS THEREFORE MUST BE DIFFERENT FROM THE WORLD THEY ARE CALLED TO INFLUENCE."
> **– JOHN MACARTHUR**

Whoa. That's convicting. We cannot influence the world when we are living like the world. God has called Christians to be influencers, and we cannot live up to His purpose for our lives if we are living like the world.

Consider This . . .
- Are you influencing the world or living like the world?

- In what areas of your life are you living like the world? (What about your thoughts, what you look at on the internet, the things that interest you, the words you use when you talk with your friends, etc.)

- What needs to change in your life so that you can influence the world?

WEEK 18
the RESCUE

WEEK 18 DAY 1

"Pray then like this: Our Father in Heaven hallowed be your name." - Matthew 6:9

In a perfect world, a father is a person who offers security, guidance, direction, and most of all...love! Although our life on earth is far from perfect, this is the kind of Father that we have once we have been rescued through Christ and sealed in the Spirit. There are many places in Scripture that help us understand this, but Jesus Himself showed us how to approach our heavenly Dad when we need Him most.

Read Matthew 6:5-13.

There is a lot we can learn from Jesus' prayer, but for now, let's focus on the fact that He modeled for us how to come to God. Jesus doesn't mean "repeat after me" when He says, "pray like this." So what does He mean? First, we are to come to God like His children...because we are! Jesus instructs us to value the family intimacy and privacy that we have with our Father. We don't need fancy words or special occasions. We can come to Him with anything!

If you follow the rest of His prayer, you can see a model that looks a little like this:
- Respect the Father
- Desire His will
- Humbly bring your needs to Him
- Depend on His help

This may seem oversimplified, but what if we really prayed like this?

Take a few minutes to look at this model and write out a prayer to your Heavenly Father that follows a pattern like this.

How different would your life be if you had an intimate time with God like this every day?

WEEK 18
DAY 2

Take a few minutes and look around your house. Do you have many family heirlooms? Some families really value passing on things like furniture, jewelry, books and other material possessions. Some cling more to family photos or old letters. Some don't really hold on to the physical items, but value family phrases or ideals.

How about your family? Can you think of any items or ideas that have been passed down in your family?

If not, what things or values do you plan to pass down that you have learned from your parents?

Regardless of the legacy you have inherited from your family, you have a legacy of faith to pass on to future generations. If you had to sum up what you believe and intend to pass on, could you do it?

Try this activity. In the space below, see if you can write one sentence that sums up what you believe about each of these topics:

The origin of life:

The nature of humans:

The character of God:

The answer to sin:

The person of Jesus Christ:

The purpose of the Bible:

This is your legacy. As children of God, we get to receive His goodness and share it with the world. Thank Him for that and ask Him to show you who you can share it with this week!

the RESCUE

WEEK 18 DAY 3

Psalm 89:26 says:
And He will cry out to me, "You are my Father, my God, the Rock my Savior."

Those are pretty powerful words! What if we could start everyday with that kind of confidence, trusting in our God, our Father, our Rock? We can, but it takes some spiritual focus to cling to a truth this big and let go of other ideas and fears that distract us.

Consider this activity to help you focus on God as your Father each morning. In the space below, take the words of this verse and create a Scripture image. Not very creative? You can do an Internet search for **"Scripture doodles"** and see lots of examples to get you started. You can also search the popular new trend of **"Bible journaling"** and get some ideas there.

Take this truth from God's Word and create an image that you can mentally carry with you throughout the day. Before you head out for the day, let these words sink in and live a BIG day as a child of God!

week 19

the RESCUE

the RESCUE

week 19 day 1

"Yet we know that a person is not justified by works of the law but through faith in Jesus Christ, so we also have believed in Christ Jesus, in order to be justified by faith in Christ and not by works of the law, because by works of the law no one will be justified." - Galatians 2:16

Have you ever looked at a task and concluded that it was impossible? Maybe it seemed impossible for you to pass chemistry. Maybe it was a physical feat that seemed impossible, like climbing a mountain.

Read Galatians 2:16.

The point is that it is impossible to be in right standing with God by obeying God's law. Why? Because no person, not a single one, is able to perfectly obey God's law. We all fall short. We can't be justified by our own obedience to the law.

But, Jesus accomplished what seemed impossible. Through His death He provided a way for us to be justified, or to be declared righteous. The way is not through our obedience to God's laws, but through our faith, or trust, in Jesus.

Consider This . . .
· How would you define faith? How is faith in Jesus different than trying to earn perfection?

· What does it mean to you personally that by trusting in Jesus you declare to be in right standing with God?

· How does this glorious truth intersect your life?

Today, let the wonder of what Jesus accomplished on the cross on your behalf permeate everything you do, say, and think.

week 19 DAY 2

Read this quote and think about the questions that follow:

"The gospel came to you because it was heading to someone else. God never intended for your salvation to be an end, but a beginning. God saved you to be a conduit through whom His glorious, life-changing gospel would flow to others." – Robby Gallaty, *Growing Up: How to Be a Disciple Who Makes Disciples*

What a powerful thought! You heard about Jesus in order that other people would hear about Jesus. The Gospel was made known to you so that you could pass it on to others.

Consider This . . .

- What is the difference between viewing your salvation as an end and viewing it as a beginning?

- What does Gallaty mean that we are to be a conduit? How do you think that looks in everyday life?

- How can you be a conduit of God's grace today?

the RESCUE

week 19 : DAY 3

In our study this past week, you were challenged to do two things. First, you were asked to read Romans 5:1 every morning as a reminder that you have a right relationship with God because of Jesus' death on the cross. Second, you were to begin praying for a friend who doesn't know Jesus and look for an opportunity to talk to him or her about it.

Today, let's take it a step further. As you walk through your school, place of employment, or favorite shopping center, pray for the people you see.

Ask God to make the Gospel known to them. Ask Him to justify them freely by His grace. Remember, at one time you stood guilty before God but now you have been declared not guilty. Pray God would do the same in their lives.

WEEK TWENTY

the RESCUE

the RESCUE

WEEK *TWENTY* DAY 1

"Speak to the entire assembly of Israel and say to them: 'Be holy because I, the LORD your God, am holy.'" - *Leviticus 19:2*

Do you have a favorite sports team? If so it's probably safe to assume you have some gear with your team's logo on it. If you're like most fans, it's more than just a hat. You probably have several hats, a couple of shirts, a few pics on your phone, and maybe even a jersey.

What is it about our teams that cause us to want to be so closely identified with them? Our identification with a team says something about our identity. There is something about who we are wrapped up in whom we pull for.

Read Leviticus 19:2. This is the very principle God was getting at. When God ordered Moses to tell the Israelites to be holy, God had one thing in mind: identity. God wanted His people to stand out from the nations around them. Not for their sake, for His. God wanted His people to be identified as people after His heart.

In essence, God was commanding His children to wear His team colors. But instead of clothing, the logo they would present to the world would be "worn" through their words, their hearts, and their actions. How about you? Do you identify yourself with God?

Consider This . . .
· Your cap or jacket says which team you pull for. Think about your actions today. What did they say to the world about how strongly you are identified with God?

· Your identification with God starts with your heart. What steps can you take to create a heart that's holy, and set-apart as God's? What changes do you need to make?

the RESCUE

WEEK TWENTY
DAY 2

At this point in your study of The Rescue, you've talked some about the new purpose that awaits those whom God rescues from sin through faith in His Son, Jesus. You also talked last week about the idea that those who are rescued are seen as forgiven in God's eyes. In this lesson, you learned to take these concepts a little deeper through a solid look at the concept of sanctification.

It's a really awesome theological truth that most of us don't really learn about until we're older. But it's such an empowering concept!

You were chosen by God to be made holy in order to be used by God to do the work of God. How powerful is that truth!? Look below at the three circles.

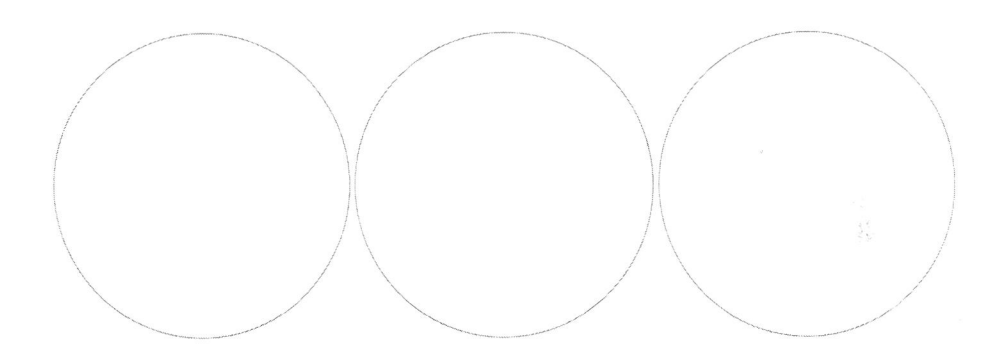

○ ○ ○

Under the first one, write the word "Home." This represents your family life. Under the second one, write the word, "School." This represents the time you spend each day at school. Under the third one write the word, "Other." This can represent your involvement with extracurricular activities or just hanging out with your friends.

God sees you as holy, to be used by Him. For each of these circles, write two or three ways this changes the way you interact with what's represented in each of these circles. When you've finished, send time in prayer thanking God that He called you to Himself to be His child, and to be used to grow His Kingdom.

82

the RESCUE

WEEK TWENTY
DAY 3

Take a moment and read this quote:

"The place God calls you to is the place where your deep gladness and the world's deep hunger meet." - Frederick Buechner, *Wishful Thinking: A Theological ABC*

Consider This . . .

- We tend to think that when God calls us to His mission, He calls us to abandon our personalities, our dreams, and so on. What does this quote say that maybe helps us rethink this idea?

- God has chosen you to be used by Him. Yet God has given you a personality, passions, talents, and past experiences. How do you think God can uses these for His glory?

- Take some time to pray to God and thank Him for making you exactly who you are. Then, ask Him to show you ways He can use your passions and talents to bring people closer to Him.

WEEK 21

the RESCUE

the **RESCUE**

WEEK 21
DAY 1

"For he himself is our peace, who has made the two groups one and has destroyed the barrier, the dividing wall of hostility, by setting aside in his flesh the law with its commands and regulations. His purpose was to create in himself one new humanity out of the two, thus making peace, and in one body to reconcile both of them to God through the cross, by which he put to death their hostility." - Ephesians 2:14-16

You see it all the time at school; people, for some reason, just don't seem to get along. Students get mad at their peers over sports or popularity or dating issues. Sometimes groups of people get mad at other groups at school. Do you ever wish these individuals and groups would just learn to get along?

At one time there was a tension between God and humankind. Our sinful nature created a barrier and a type of hostility in the spiritual realm. The passage you just read has two great points:

- God initiated the reconciliation with humans due to our sin. Jesus allowed us to once again be one with God.
- His remedy is always peace. We are at peace with God and we can be at peace with other people.

Consider This . . .
· There is an old saying that goes something like this, "Have you made your peace with God"? That actually means, "Have you discovered the peace that comes from a right relationship with God?" How would you describe that peace?

· In the lesson this past week you learned that God has called you to be a minister of reconciliation. Do you think that has anything to do with being a peacemaker at your school? What could you do to help people reconcile their differences at your school?

WEEK 21 DAY 2

Read this quote:

"A WISE MAN WHO KNOWS PROVERBS CAN RECONCILE DIFFICULTIES."
- ANONYMOUS

Have you ever spent much time reading the Old Testament book of Proverbs? The man who wrote most of the book was King Solomon and he was very good at reconciling people in their relationships. Look at one of his sayings from Proverbs 17: 9:

"LOVE PROSPERS WHEN A FAULT IS FORGIVEN, BUT DWELLING ON IT SEPARATES CLOSE FRIENDS."

Consider gaining a better understanding of the word "reconciliation" by reading through the book of Proverbs. You will soon see the power of forgiveness when it comes to living at peace with people in this world and serving as an ambassador of reconciliation. Always be slow to anger and quick to forgive.

the **RESCUE**

WEEK 21 DAY 3

"Since God chose you to be the holy people he loves, you must clothe yourselves with tenderhearted mercy, kindness, humility, gentleness, and patience. Make allowance for each other's faults, and forgive anyone who offends you. Remember, the Lord forgave you, so you must forgive others. Above all, clothe yourselves with love, which binds us all together in perfect harmony. And let the peace that comes from Christ rule in your hearts. For as members of one body you are called to live in peace. And always be thankful." - Colossians 3:12-15

Let's break down these awesome verses. As holy people loved by God, what are six things the apostle Paul tells believers to make sure are parts of their daily character? Write the answer in the space below:

And as forgiven people what should we be doing when it comes to our relationships with others?

What will rule our hearts when we live out these verses each day?

Notice the little bombshell at the very end of the passage. Always be what?

Meditate on these verses then ask God let your character not just reflect but BE what is described in the passage from Colossians.

WEEK 22
the RESCUE

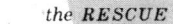

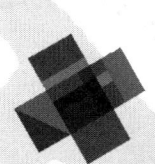

WEEK 22 DAY 1

"When Christ who is your life appears, then you also will appear with him in glory."
- Colossians 3:4

What if Jesus came back today? Your life as you know it would be over. The things that we often think matter so deeply — grades, dating relationships, athletic achievements, and social status — would be gone in an instant. They would be seen as the short-term and temporary things that they are. What would matter in the moment that Jesus returns is what will truly matter.

Read Colossians 3:4.

Paul says that Jesus is our life and that one day we will experience that true life in Him. The question is: are we living our TODAY for that ONE DAY? Because the reality is that the Bible says that Jesus will come in a moment when we least expect it, and that moment could be today.

Time is ticking away. Your life matters for eternity. Are you making your today count for that day?

Consider This . . .
· How are you going to make today count for that one day?

· If today was your last day before Jesus came back, whom do you need to share Him with so that they could experience that one day too?

WEEK 22
DAY 2

Go back and re-read the passage you studied this week, Colossians 3:1-4. The cool thing is that we see several word pictures:

- Raised with Christ. (v. 1)
- Christ, seated at the right hand of God. (v. 1)
- Set your minds on things above. (v. 2)
- You have died. (v. 3)
- Your life is hidden with Christ in God. (v. 3)
- When Christ, your life, appears. (v. 4)

Using the space below, take one of these word pictures above and express it creatively. You could draw a picture of what you imagine that looking like. You could write a poem around the theme of the image. You could write a prayer to God praising Him for being that for you.

Once you complete your creative expression, take a picture of it and make it your phone's home screen as a reminder to you of the importance of living in light of heavenly priorities.

WEEK 22 DAY 3

In the space provided below, take some time today to journal about what you think it will be like when you meet Jesus face-to-face.

Use this time to encourage your heart that meeting Jesus is the moment you have been living, waiting, and longing for.

Use it as a time to set your heart and mind on things above versus things of this earth.

week 23

the RESCUE

the **RESCUE**

week 23 | day 1

"Dear friends, I urge you, as foreigners and exiles, to abstain from sinful desires, which wage war against your soul." - 1 Peter 2:11

Think about your bedroom at your house. What have you done to make it your room? How have you decorated it? What do you keep there that's just yours and no one else's? You probably have taken at least some time to get your room the way you want it.

Now, think about this: When you stay in a hotel or go on a retreat or to a camp, do you put as much effort into redecorating your room? Sure, you might bring a picture or two if you will be there for a while, but you don't change everything as if you're going to be there for years, right?

Read 1 Peter 2:11.

Peter says that if we follow Jesus, we are foreigners in this world. (Some translations say "temporary residents.") This world really is not our home. It's like we're staying at a hotel for a while before we get to our true home.

God wants you to love your true home more than this temporary one. It's not that there's nothing good here; after all, God created it, didn't He? But we are not meant to be here forever, so we shouldn't be attached to this world and everything in it—especially to those things that aren't really what God wants for us.

Consider This . . .
· What is one thing about this world that you're glad is not a part of God's Kingdom?

· Think back to the Bible study from this week. What was the one thing you chose to let go of from this world? How's it going?

the RESCUE

week 23
DAY 2

This week, we talked about God's Kingdom and how Jesus rescued us into His Kingdom.

Take one minute—yep, set a timer on your phone for 60 seconds—and, using the space provided below, write a quick letter to God about what you like about His Kingdom.

No one else will read it, so don't worry about how it sounds. Just start writing and don't stop until 60 seconds is up.

Ready? Go.

week 23 DAY 3

We often spend a lot of time thinking about what God has rescued us to—His Kingdom—rather than what He has rescued us from.

Think about one part of this world that has caused you pain or sadness. It could be something that happened to you, or it could be something that you've done that you know you shouldn't have.

That pain and sadness is part of what Jesus rescued you from when he rescued you into His Kingdom from the "dominion of darkness."

Now, spend about 2 minutes in prayer simply thanking God that he has rescued you from that dominion into the kingdom of His Son, where one day there will be no more pain. You can write your prayer in the space below if that helps you.

WEEK

TWENTY-FOUR

the RESCUE

WEEK TWENTY-FOUR DAY 1

"But the Helper, the Holy Spirit, whom the Father will send in my name, he will teach you all things and bring to your remembrance all that I have said to you." - John 14:26

Have you ever forgotten someone's name? Maybe you were right in the middle of an introduction when disaster happened. "This is Stew." "And Stew, this is . . . uhhhh . . ." Embarrassing, right? It happens to the best of us.

Read John 14:26.

Can you imagine how the disciples must have felt when Jesus told them that He wanted them to make disciples, just like He had made them into disciples? "Wait! What? You want us to do what you did? I can't even remember half of what you taught and I'm supposed to teach someone else?" I'm sure they were panicked. Remembering people's names can be difficult, how much more difficult would it be to remember three years of Jesus' teaching?

The solution, though, is that Jesus promised His disciples (and us) the Holy Spirit. One of the jobs of the Holy Spirit is to help disciples remember the words of the Master. One of the great benefits to having the Holy Spirit living inside us is that He will bring to our minds truth we've learned about God. He will also continue to teach us. So, when you are struggling to understand, that is a great time to ask the Spirit to make it clear for you.

Consider This . . .
· Have you ever had the Holy Spirit help you remember a teaching of Jesus when you needed it?

· How is knowing that God will continue to teach you and remind you of His truth a source of comfort?

· Why do we need the Holy Spirit do help us learn and remember?

WEEK TWENTY-FOUR

DAY 2

Check out this quote from Francis Chan:

"If it's true that the Spirit of God dwells in us and that our bodies are the Holy Spirit's temple, then shouldn't there be a huge difference between the person who has the Spirit of God living inside of him or her and the person who does not?" -Francis Chan, *Forgotten God: Reversing Our Tragic Neglect of the Holy Spirit*

That's a great question. Here are a couple more to help you process this quote.

Consider This . . .
· What difference should the Holy Spirit living inside of us make in our everyday lives?

· How do you see the Holy Spirit at work in your own life? What difference is He making in you?

· Make an honest evaluation of your life today. Do you see outward actions that confirm the inward reality of the presence of God's Spirit in your life?

the RESCUE

WEEK TWENTY-FOUR
DAY 3

In this week's lesson we examined the fruit of the Spirit in Galatians 5:22-23. Remember, the fruit of the Spirit are characteristics or traits that the Spirit of God produces in the lives of believers. They are love, joy, peace, patience, kindness, goodness, faithfulness, gentleness, and self-control.

Here is your mission today: Use your phone to document how you see these traits in action.

You could take a picture of someone sharing as an example of kindness. You could take a picture of an older couple holding hands as an example of faithfulness. You could take a picture of verses that describe joy.

Be creative!

The key is to spend today looking for examples of the Holy Spirit at work around you.

WEEK 25
the RESCUE

the **RESCUE**

WEEK 25
DAY 1

"And Jesus came and said to them, 'All authority in heaven and on earth has been given to me. Go therefore and make disciples of all nations, baptizing them in the name of the Father and of the Son and of the Holy Spirit, teaching them to observe all that I have commanded you. And behold, I am with you always, to the end of the age.'" - Matthew 28:18-20

We discussed how the Great Commission is the mission of every Christian. Hopefully, our discussion of the passage made it clear what Jesus has commanded believers to do. As it is our life's mission, spend some time meditating on the passage.

In fact, go write it down. That's right. Use the space below to write down the passage word for word. If you're artistic, decorate it.

Now, read it aloud. Seriously. Read the passage aloud three or four times. The goal is to have the words of this passage ringing in your head and heart all day.

It's one of the true defining commands of Christ-followers. You can't focus on it too much!

the **RESCUE**

WEEK 25 DAY 2

"While walking by the Sea of Galilee, he [Jesus] saw two brothers, Simon (who is called Peter) and Andrew his brother, casting a net into the sea, for they were fishermen. And he said to them, 'Follow me, and I will make you fishers of men.' Immediately they left their nets and followed him." - Matthew 4:18-20

Peter and Andrew were fishermen. We can assume they likely were good at it and that they enjoyed it since they had chosen it for a profession. Think about what you enjoy doing. What are you good at? List these things below:

1.

2.

3.

4.

5.

Jesus used unique fishing terminology to share what he wanted Peter and Andrew to do in the future: fish for men. He wanted them to share the good news of salvation with others. Contemplate how you can use the activities you enjoy and the things that you are good at to reach people for Christ. Also, consider the fact that as soon as Jesus gave Peter and Andrew a mission, they dropped their nets and followed Him. Peter and Andrew must have decided that Jesus' mission for them (to fish for men) was of greater value than their current mission (to fish for a living). Ask yourself, "Am I willing to go and do whatever Jesus asks of me?"

the **RESCUE**

WEEK 25 DAY 3

We see in the Great Commission that we are to make disciples, baptize, and teach wherever we are and wherever we go. Think of one way that you can use social media today to teach others about Jesus. The sky is the limit. Some ideas are listed below to get you thinking. Of course, if you cannot think of a better idea, feel free to use one of these.

· Post a picture of a Bible passage (such as Matthew 28:18-20) or list your status as spending time with God.

· Check in at your local church and invite others to join you.

· If God has brought specific people to mind to pray for their salvation, send them a private message telling them you are praying for them. Encourage them to continue to seek truth. (Then make sure you are following through with praying for them.)

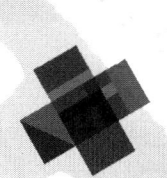

the RESCUE

WEEK 26
the RESCUE

WEEK 26 DAY 1

"And without faith it is impossible to please God, because anyone who comes to him must believe that he exists and that he rewards those who earnestly seek him." - Hebrews 11:6

Have you ever had a Reward Card? You know, one of those cards that you get punched when you buy a sub and after 10 you get 1 free? Or maybe a card that gives you $10 off a purchase when you spend $100 at a store? These cards are a way for stores to keep you coming back over and over again to spend and spend some more.

Did you know that as a Christian you have one of the greatest Reward Cards? Now while we do not serve God just for the rewards, the writer of Hebrews says that God will reward those who earnestly seek Him. Well some pretty smart people known as theologians have broken down the whole verse and come up with this: the reward is God; His presence today and our future life with Him.

Now that is a great Reward Card, one we get to enjoy now and forever and one that was paid in full when Jesus died for us on the cross!

WEEK 26
DAY 2

Jesus answered, "I am the way and the truth and the life. No one comes to the Father except through me." - John 14:6

You may have read this verse before. But read it again. What does it make you think about?

Have you encountered anyone in your life that would disagree with this? What would he or she say is an alternative way to heaven?

Here's the deal: You're going to run into people who think that because you live your life according to God's Word, and because Jesus said that He is the only means to gain access to God and heaven, that you are close minded. That you are hateful. That you are unintelligent and uninformed.

Why do you think people react this way to Jesus?

As a Christ-follower, what's the proper response to people who might react this way? What is your role in answering their questions but also showing them the grace and kindness of God?

the RESCUE

WEEK 26 DAY 3

Take a moment and read this simple quote:

"OUR DUTY AS CHRISTIANS IS ALWAYS TO KEEP HEAVEN IN OUR EYE AND THE EARTH UNDER OUR FEET."
- MATTHEW HENRY

Consider This . . .
· We talked in our lesson about the idea of how heaven, and a future life with Christ, can encourage and empower us in this life. How does what Henry says here relate to that?

· How does keeping "heaven in your eye" change the way you see this life?
Lines for writing

· What is the problem with not keeping one eye on our future with God? What impact can this have on the way we live our lives on this earth?

week 27

the RESCUE

the RESCUE

week 27 day 1

"For I am not ashamed of the gospel, for it is the power of God for salvation to everyone who believes, to the Jew first and also to the Greek." - Romans 1:16

In 1878, Oxford University Professor Erasmus Wilson said, "When the Paris Exhibition closes, electric light will close with it and no more will be heard of it." Similarly, the president of a bank advised Henry Ford's lawyer to refuse to invest in Ford Motor Company because, "The horse is here to stay but the automobile is only a novelty, a fad." Needless to say, electricity and automobiles seemed mighty foolish to many people at the time of their inventions.

Read Romans 1:16. Paul stated that he was not ashamed of the Gospel. Because of its power to impact lives, he was, in fact, proud to proclaim it to everyone who would listen so that they might believe. Now, read 1 Corinthians 1:20-25. In the face of long-standing Jewish tradition and pagan religions (which did not believe anything near Judaism) Christianity looked foolish. Paul admitted to the church in Corinth that the news of Christ's death and resurrection was not exactly welcome words to many. It seemed foolish to place one's faith in the belief that a man who had died was also raised to life again and was actually the Son of God. Paul stated, though, that this was God's wise plan, and he was proud to preach it.

When we know the truth of the Gospel, we can rest assured that even though others may think we are foolish, we can proclaim it without hesitation. Although we don't know what may happen tomorrow, we do know God's ultimate plan to redeem His children. Just as electricity never went away, we can be confident that what some find foolish today will ultimately prove to be truth to all.

Consider This . . .
- What gives you the most hesitation when opportunities to share the Gospel come up?

- What would you need to be able to say that you were proud to proclaim the Gospel of Christ to others who do not yet believe?

week 27 DAY 2

Social media has become a great place to share photos, life events, or even just quick thoughts. But it can also be a place where we seek out approval. When we post a picture or a thought, we expect responses. While the negative ones affect us more greatly than we admit, the positive "like[s]" and "love[s]" and comments are what we really look for. In a way, they validate us and the life we want to portray (even if it isn't completely our real lives).

Be honest, sometimes do you imagine that God has a little button that He pushes every time you attempt to do something for Him? Nothing is wrong with wanting to please God through our obedience to Him, but we don't earn His favor with "good" works. If we are His children, He loves us. Period.

As you view or post pictures or life events on social media this week, think about your motivation before God.

Not only is our virtual life not a representation of our true value in God's sight, it's also not a representation of our standing before God. If you are a Christ follower, you are His, and your walk with Him is based completely on what He has already done for you. Think about this truth today. Contemplate it and talk to God about it in prayer. Listen to what He has to say to you in return.

week 27 DAY 3

If you are a follower of Christ, take heart; you can do nothing good enough to earn God's love and nothing bad enough for Him to abandon you!

Think about that truth.

How does that lift burdens you've placed on yourself?

How does it motivate you to respond in love?

Using the space below, take a couple of minutes to write 2-3 sentences to God, thanking Him for providing everything you need to be restored to Him.

WEEK TWENTY-EIGHT

the RESCUE

the RESCUE

WEEK *TWENTY-EIGHT* DAY 1

"And how are they to preach unless they are sent? As it is written, 'How beautiful are the feet of those who preach the good news!'" – Romans 10:15

There are two great obstacles that people face in sharing their faith. FIRST, many are not sure who to share it with. If Scripture tells us we are "sent," then we are sent somewhere specific. Wherever God has planted you, there are people for you to reach.

Take a minute and ask God to put someone on your heart that needs to hear about Him. Pray specifically for that person to be ready to hear.

SECOND, most don't know how to begin a conversation about spiritual things. The easiest way is to be familiar with your own encounter with Christ. Even if you were saved at a young age, there was a time when you realized that you didn't know Christ and wanted to. This is your story. Take some time to write it out in your own words. Grab some paper or your computer and jot down your thoughts. It doesn't need to be long. It doesn't matter so much when and where as what you understood to be true. Think about it in these three parts:

1. **What you realized you were missing?** Was it purpose, a relationship with your Creator, love, belonging, forgiveness, etc.? What sparked your awareness that you needed Jesus?

2. **What did you believe and do?** This is where you can use verses that you've learned about salvation. Here is where you want to focus on Jesus as the solution to your separation from God.

3. **How has your life been different since that decision?** This is where you share what Jesus means to you now. How does knowing Christ make your life worth living? In other words, why should they want what you have?

the **RESCUE**

WEEK TWENTY-EIGHT
DAY 2

Have you ever noticed advertisements or signs for disaster preparedness? Depending on where you live, there may be seasonal public service programs to get people ready for hurricanes, floods, earthquakes, zombie apocalypse, whatever! The point is always the same: you need to prepare BEFORE the situation arises. The same is true for sharing your faith. Today, you are going to spend a few minutes to prepare your own "EVANGELISM PREPAREDNESS" kit.

By now, you may already have the 3 Circles app downloaded. If not, take a moment and do so.

You should have already written out your own story of how Christ changed your life.

Now you need to have some Scripture handy to share to back up your personal experience.

Grab your Bible and a highlighter or colored pencil. Find each of these verses and highlight them in your Bible. Choose one to write on a 3 x 5 card or sticky note to place in a visible place. Commit to memorize this verse. When it's done, choose another until you have them all!

- John 3:16-17
- Romans 3:23
- Romans 5:8
- Romans 6:23
- Romans 10:9

Add any others that you may find helpful to the list.

the RESCUE

WEEK TWENTY-EIGHT
DAY 3

Take a few minutes and read back over Romans chapter 10. There is so much truth packed into this short chapter. Now, consider doing something brave. Really, really brave! Right now, think of one person that you could contact today to share what you have been practicing this week. If you know someone who needs to hear the message of Jesus, that would be the perfect person to choose. If God hasn't laid anyone on your heart, you can always practice on a family member or church friend just to get comfortable. Either way, take a verbal step to try this for real!

Say something like:
- Hey, at my church we have been talking about how to share what we really believe with other people. Everybody believes something, but sometimes it's hard to put it into words. They challenged us to think it through and share it with someone this week. Can I try to share with you just a few minutes and see if I can explain it clearly?

If this makes you nervous, that's totally normal. Don't let it stop you. You've got this! More importantly, God's got you!!! Give it a try, you just might preach the words someone needs to believe!

WEEK 29
the RESCUE

the **RESCUE**

WEEK 29
DAY 1

"Because, if you confess with your mouth that Jesus is Lord and believe in your heart that God raised him from the dead, you will be saved." - Romans 10:9

Everyone is always looking for the easy way out. How do I get a good grade on this test without studying? How can I turn in this assignment with the least effort possible? Is homework really necessary?

The reality is that the two things that Paul calls us to do in this passage are so much more than magic words or a shortcut to faith. It's 100% true that belief in Christ saves us. But to really confess that Jesus is Lord means that we've decided that we're not in control of our lives anymore, and we've handed the keys over to Jesus. If we *really* believe that Jesus came back to life - that changes everything!

Sometimes we can think Christianity is just saying or thinking the right things. And then we get to go on living however we want. But if we really look at what Paul is calling us to do, we realize that it's more than just words and thoughts. If we really believe Jesus is who He says He is, we will live differently. Our belief is a transforming belief. We no longer live for ourselves, but we live for Him!

Consider This . . .
· Have you done this? Do you believe in Christ and have you confessed it with your mouth? If you have, spend some time thanking God for His saving you. If you haven't, take some time to think about why. Consider talking to your church leader or parents about your questions.

· Think about the last phrase of this passage: "Everyone who believes in Him will not be put to shame." What do you think that means? If we believe in Him, Jesus will not abandon us when we need Him, but He provides us with life everlasting!

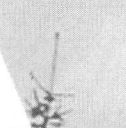

the RESCUE

WEEK 29 DAY 2

The verse we looked at this week talked about the importance of saying and really believing that "Jesus is Lord." Check out this verse from another letter that Paul wrote in the New Testament:

"Therefore I want you to understand that no one speaking in the Spirit of God ever says 'Jesus is accursed!' and no one can say 'Jesus is Lord' except in the Holy Spirit." - 1 Corinthians 12:3

In the first part of that verse, Paul is simply saying that Christians don't speak against Jesus. Think about the second part of the verse: "no one can say 'Jesus is Lord' except in the Holy Spirit." Basically, we need God to find God!

Consider This . . .
· If no one can say, "Jesus is Lord" without the help of the Holy Spirit, we know that it's not just us looking for salvation, but God is calling people to Himself! Do you know anyone who isn't a Christian? Think of some friends that you wish could know Jesus.

· Spend some time praying for them by name. Pray that God would call them to Himself through the Holy Spirit. Pray that Holy Spirit would give them the courage to say and really believe that "Jesus is Lord."

· You might pray that God would even use you to be a part of that! How can you share the truth of Jesus- *that He died for us*- with your friends?

the **RESCUE**

WEEK 29 DAY 3

When did you become a Christian? Try to think back to that moment.

What where you thinking?

What where you struggling with?

Why did you respond to Jesus in that moment?

Remember this verse from our lesson this week:

"For the Scripture says, 'Everyone who believes in him will not be put to shame.'"
- Romans 10:11

Think about that. Because you have placed your faith in Christ, you will not be put to shame!

That means...
- You will not be separated from God forever because of your sin.
- You will live forever together with Christ!
- You will not be judged based on your own works, but on the works of Christ! Because of Jesus, you will be seen by God as holy and blameless!
- You get to live a life of faith even now! God has a personal calling for you.

Spend some time in prayer thanking Jesus for His sacrifice. Thank God for loving you enough to send Jesus for you. Thank the Holy Spirit for helping you see Jesus and proclaim with your mouth and your life that "Jesus is Lord."

the RESCUE

WEEK
30
the RESCUE

WEEK 30 DAY 1

"To the weak I became weak, that I might win the weak. I have become all things to all people, that by all means I might save some. I do it all for the sake of the gospel, that I may share with them in its blessings." - 1 Corinthians 9:22-23

Have you ever felt out of place? Awkward? Out of your comfort zone? What situations make you feel like that? Why is it scary for you to venture into unfamiliar situations or circumstances?

Paul knew what it was like to feel awkward. He knew what it was like to be stretched, mocked, and uncomfortable. He said earlier in 1 Corinthians 9 that he went everywhere and anywhere to help people understand Christ. If it were up to him, he probably would have not gone out of his comfort zone. Going out of our comfort zone and being willing to do what's best for others is difficult and awkward, and we usually don't like it. Yet, Paul knew that what was more important than his feelings was the message that God gave him to share. Paul knew that, no matter what, there were people living without Jesus, and that simply wasn't ok.

Consider This . . .
· What do you think it would take for you to be willing to do "whatever" to get the good news of Jesus to people?

· Are there some people that are just too hard for you to even consider spending time with for the sake of Christ? Why or why not?

WEEK 30
DAY 2

Do you remember the index cards you wrote on during Bible Study this week? On one side of the card you wrote things that keep you from sharing the good news with everyone and anyone. On the other side you wrote one thing you would do about that.

Today, take out that card (or spend time recreating it) and then take the time to write a letter to the Lord. Ask Him to show you what people you need to reach out to for the sake of Jesus. Ask Him to show you what holds you back. Finally, ask Him for an idea of one thing you can do to reach out to those people.

Once you have done that "one thing," use the space below to write what you did and what happened as a result of reaching beyond your comfort zone for Jesus.

the RESCUE

WEEK 30 DAY 3

Today, take a few moments to ask God why feeling uncomfortable often wins out over spending time bringing His message to those who need it.

Ask the Lord to help you see someone who is hurting today and change your attitude toward helping him or her.

Write your prayer in the space below:

week 31

the RESCUE

the RESCUE

week 31 day 1

"'My food,'" said Jesus, 'is to do the will of him who sent me and to finish his work. Don't you have a saying, "It's still four months until harvest"? I tell you, open your eyes and look at the fields! They are ripe for harvest. Even now the one who reaps draws a wage and harvests a crop for eternal life, so that the sower and the reaper may be glad together. Thus the saying "One sows and another reaps" is true. I sent you to reap what you have not worked for. Others have done the hard work, and you have reaped the benefits of their labor.'" - John 4:34-38

Assembly line workers at an auto plant have a wide variety of jobs. Some people assemble the various parts that go on the car. Others put on the doors or add the windows to the vehicle. Jobs can range from something as small as adding screws and bolts to as big as adding tires. The end result is a new car or truck that rolls off the assembly line, ready to be sent to a dealership to sell.

Lots of people add their particular skill to the production of a car, but only one person gets to drive the finished product off the assembly line. In the passage you just read, Jesus used the analogy of a crop being ready to harvest to explain the process of a person coming to a point when they make a decision to accept Christ. Your encouragement to someone, your invitation to church or to a youth camp, or sharing the Gospel may be part of the process that leads a person to salvation even though you may not actually see the person get saved. Whether you plant a seed or get to see an actual "harvest," each part of the process is important in a person's journey to salvation.

Consider This . . .

· Have you been actively investing in the salvation process of others by sharing the Gospel this week?

· Are you content being just a small part of the process of someone coming to know Jesus?

· Remember that no small thing ever done in the name of Christ comes back void. The Holy Spirit takes all of our words and deeds done in the name of Jesus and plants them in the lives of others.

week 31 DAY 2

What is the thirstiest you've ever been? Can you remember it? What was it like when you finally got to drink some water?

In our lesson this week, Jesus offered the woman at the well "living water." Our bodies are desperate for water. We must have it for survival. When we don't have it, we crave it. Our bodies long for it.

Spend some time thinking about your relationship with Christ. Do you crave Him in the same way your body needs water? Do you long for Him? Is your relationship with Him refreshing and life giving?

Then, take some time and consider how your heart can be stirred to long for Jesus more than anything else in this world. Record any thoughts in the space below:

the RESCUE

week 31 | DAY 3

For the past five weeks you have been focusing on the power of the Gospel and sharing the Gospel with others. What about your story? How did you come to the point when you put your faith in Jesus Christ? Who are some of the people who shared the Gospel with you over the years? Take a few minutes to jot down the answers to these questions and you will see how different people over the years helped you come to your moment of salvation.

Now, take a minute to thank God for all of these people who shared the Gospel with you. Ask God to help you be part of someone else's journey to the cross.

WEEK THIRTY-TWO

the RESCUE

WEEK THIRTY-TWO DAY 1

"But I say to you that everyone who is angry with his brother will be liable to judgment; whoever insults his brother will be liable to the council; and whoever says, 'You fool!' will be liable to the hell of fire." - Matthew 5:22

Slamming doors. Pounding fists. Clinched jaws. Screaming mouths. Insulting words. Chilly silence. How do you respond when something or someone makes you angry?

Read Matthew 5:22. Although anger is an emotion that we have all experienced, Jesus says that those who are angry with their brother and those who act in anger deserve judgment and hell. Jesus is talking about an anger that sits in the heart and seeks revenge. He is emphasizing that those who have been rescued to God's kingdom, have no place for this type of anger in their lives. We cannot let anger sit in our hearts, control our thoughts and lead our actions. There is a better way.

God has placed the Holy Spirit in the heart of every member of His kingdom. If you have been rescued from sin and death through faith in Christ, you have been given the Spirit to help you respond with love and grace in any situation. No matter what has been done to you, you do not have to let anger rule your life. Through His power, you do not have to respond in anger. You can allow God's Word to rule in your heart, Christ to control your thoughts, and the Holy Spirit to lead your actions.

The next time something causes your temper to flare, fight against any of your typical angry responses. Rather than responding in anger, walk according to the Spirit that lives inside you. Return blessings for curses, extend a hand in forgiveness and compassion rather than pounding your fists, sing praises rather than scream, speak words of life rather than retreating in chilly silence.

Consider This . . .
· What can happen if you allow anger to control your life rather than the Holy Spirit?

· What are some specific ways that can you replace your typical anger-driven responses with responses that honor Christ?

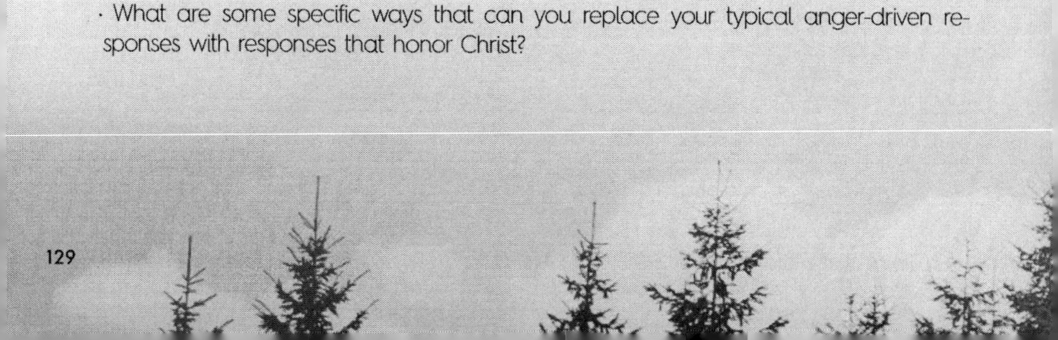

the **RESCUE**

WEEK THIRTY-TWO

DAY 2

Here is a challenge for you: In Colossians 3:9-12, followers of Jesus are told,

"You must put them all away: anger, wrath, malice, slander, and obscene talk from your mouth...you have put off the old self with its practices and have put on the new self...Put on, then, as God's chosen ones, holy and beloved, compassionate hearts, kindness, humility, meekness, and patience...above all these put on love."

This week when you change clothes, use it as time to think through this truth.

As you change out of one outfit, imagine taking off the old self and its practices and throwing it away (i.e., throw it into your dirty clothes hamper). As you dress into a new outfit, imagine putting on the new self and its practices. Think about throwing out anger, wrath, malice, slander and obscene talk and putting on compassion, kindness, humility, meekness, patience and love instead. You would not put your stinky, dirty clothes back on over your freshly washed clothes. In the same way, do not put the old self and its practices back on.

You have been rescued—dress like it!

the RESCUE

WEEK THIRTY-TWO
DAY 3

Read this quote aloud:

"ANGER IS AN ACID THAT CAN DO MORE HARM TO THE VESSEL IN WHICH IT IS STORED THAN TO ANYTHING ON WHICH IT IS POURED."
- MARK TWAIN

Consider This . . .

- How is anger like an acid? How does it cause harm?

- What are some ways that your anger has hurt you in the past?

- How can trusting Jesus more deeply impact your struggle with anger?

WEEK 33

the RESCUE

WEEK 33
DAY 1

"If your right eye causes you to stumble, gouge it out and throw it away. It is better for you to lose one part of your body than for your whole body to be thrown into hell. And if your right hand causes you to stumble, cut it off and throw it away. It is better for you to lose one part of your body than for your whole body to go into hell." – Matthew 5:29-30

Jesus calls for extreme measures for things that cause His followers to fall into lust. Though you probably shouldn't tear out your eye or cut off your arm, Jesus is using that imagery to show us that there may be some drastic measures you should take to guard yourself from lust.

Pull out your notecard from this week's lesson. Do you see a pattern in your times when you are tempted to fall into lust? Is it when you are bored? Alone? Feeling worthless? Identify the moments where you find yourself in the middle of the battle.

Is there a certain place or item that is always involved in your struggle? Does it happen during a certain time of the day at school? Does it always involve your computer, phone, or TV? Once you identify the places of the battleground, what can you do to guard your heart and actions in those moments? Are there places you don't need to go? Maybe you don't need to take your phone to bed at night. What are the safeguards you can put into your life?

Remember, as a follower of Jesus, there is no place for lust in your life. Spend some time this morning thinking of your personal battle plan.

Consider This . . .
· What is your personal battle plan?

· Share your battle plan with the battle partner (accountability partner, mentor, youth pastor, small group leader, etc.) and get their thoughts on your plan. Give them permission to hold you accountable and call you out.

· How does trusting Jesus' best for your life help you continue the fight against lust?

the **RESCUE**

WEEK 33 DAY 2

See the three crosses below. Take a moment and cut them out.

Now, put these images of the cross in the places where you are most likely to struggle with lust.

When you are tempted to fall into lust, look at the drawing or image of the cross to remind yourself that Jesus is better than the temporary satisfaction of lust.

He is the only One who truly satisfies your heart.

the RESCUE

WEEK 33 DAY 3

Take a moment and read this quote:

"LOVE IS THE GREAT CONQUEROR OF LUST."
- C. S. LEWIS, MERE CHRISTIANITY

Take a few minutes and think about that quote. Then, consider the following questions:

· How does the love of God seen in Jesus' death on the cross for you help you to conquer lust?

· What is the true understanding of love that allows you to conquer your struggle with lust?

· How can love for God motivate you to pursue purity in all areas of your life?

WEEK 34
the RESCUE

WEEK 34 DAY 1

"For to this you have been called, because Christ also suffered for you, leaving you an example, so that you might follow in his steps." - 1 Peter 2:21

All of us have been hurt by someone. Unfortunately, it's a part of life. Another part of life is revenge—at least wanting it. Be honest: have you ever imagined what it would be like to get back at someone who hurt you? Have you ever planned it out in your mind, even if you knew you'd never go through with it?

Maybe it was the so-called "friend" who ended up stabbing you in the back. Or, perhaps it was a sibling who can't ever seem to say anything nice to you. Maybe it's a teacher or a coach you'd swear has it out for you.

Have you ever wondered whether Jesus wanted revenge? I know, it's a weird thing to think about. Even if you've never asked that question, you're about to get the answer. Read 1 Peter 2:21-23. Jesus was hurt in unimaginable ways when He died on the cross for you. He suffered, and He didn't deserve even a little bit of that suffering. And, did you read what Peter said about Jesus? Jesus didn't fight back or retaliate.

One of the most painful realities of life is that people will hurt you. Sometimes even people you love. We don't get to choose when and where people will hurt us, but what we do get to choose is how we respond. Jesus invites you to follow in His steps and respond the way He did.

Consider This . . .
· Have you ever gotten revenge or retaliated against someone who hurt you? How did that feel? Did the hurt go away?

· Think back to the Bible Study from this week. What was the one area where you said you would put this week's study into practice? How's it going?

WEEK 34
DAY 2

This week we read in 1 Peter that instead of seeking revenge against those who hurt Him, Jesus entrusted Himself to God, who judges justly.

Today, you're going to practice doing that.

Pick one person who has hurt you whom you have thought about hurting back in some way.

In the space provided below, write a letter to God about that person and how they hurt you. Be honest with God about how you feel, maybe even how it is hard to trust Him in that situation.

Now, spend some time praying that God would allow you to forgive this person.

WEEK 34 DAY 3

"RESENTMENT IS LIKE DRINKING A POISON AND THEN WAITING FOR THE OTHER PERSON TO DIE."
- UNKNOWN

That's quite a take on what we heard Jesus say this week, isn't it?

Consider This . . .
- Do you think the quote is true? How have you seen it to be true in your life?

- Who is one person you are bitter or resentful toward right now?

- Do you wish you could get revenge on that person? What is that doing to your heart?

Spend some time praying for that person and asking God how you can choose to respond to this person with love instead of retaliation.

week 35

the RESCUE

the RESCUE

week 35 day 1

"Bless those who persecute you; bless and do not curse them." - Romans 12:14

People can be difficult. I mean really difficult. Most of us have people in our lives who seem like they are always against us. You know, the person who hates your idea. The person who makes fun of your shirt. The person who seems like he or she never has anything nice or encouraging to say. It's discouraging to even be in the same room with them.

Read Romans 12:14.

As we learn to live as citizens of God's Kingdom, one key component is how we treat other people, specifically people who don't treat us well. In response to persecution, citizens of God's Kingdom bless. In response to cursing, we bless. This way of life is not easy. The easy way is to tell that person why they are such a jerk face. But, God has a better way to live in mind. God's way is to respond to difficult people with grace and blessing.

Consider This . . .
- What does our response to difficult people say about our faith?

- Why is living this way so hard? Why is blessing others worth it?

- How can you be a blessing to a difficult person today?

… the RESCUE

week 35 DAY 2

Read this quote:

"Love means to love that which is unlovable; or it is no virtue at all."
- G.K. Chesterton

Wait, what? The virtue of love lies in loving the unlovable. That's deep.

Consider This . . .
- Why is love only virtuous when we are able to love the unlovable?

- How does loving people who don't deserve it display the power of love?

Today, ask God to give you an opportunity to extend love to someone who is difficult to love. Then, when you have the opportunity, seize it.

week 35 DAY 3

We talked about loving our enemies who are close to us. But, today I want you to think about people who may be enemies that are far from us.

Pull up a world map on your phone and identify a country that contains people that a lot of Americans would consider enemies. Maybe Afghanistan, Syria, Iraq, North Korea, or somewhere else.

Then, take a few minutes to pray for the people of that country. Ask God to rescue people in that country from their sins. Pray for believers who may live there and missionaries who are serving in that country. Remember that we are citizens of God's Kingdom first and foremost as you pray for your enemies.

WEEK THIRTY-SIX

the RESCUE

the RESCUE

WEEK *THIRTY-SIX* DAY 1

"Do not love the world or the things in the world. If anyone loves the world, the love of the Father is not in him." - 1 John 2:15

Do you have $20? Do you have $5? Chances are you do, or that you will at some point in the near future. Maybe you have a job. Perhaps you get an allowance. Or you might have birthday money stored somewhere.

Read 1 John 2:15-17. In this passage, the apostle John is writing to a group of early Christians. This is a great reminder for Christians today, too. It is human nature to be selfish. Most of us think of ourselves more often than we do anyone else. That makes it easy to spend money on what makes us happy without ever pausing to consider a higher purpose for our funds. Tithing (a biblical principle of giving a portion of all we have back to God first before spending the rest) is wonderful! But, did you know that God is not just interested in how much we give to Him, but also in how we choose to spend the rest we keep?

It's not to suggest that God is angry if you go to the movies and buy a large popcorn. God created joy and wants you to experience it! A fun night out with friends at the movies may be just the way to do that. But, it's OK to suggest that we not think only of ourselves and what we desire. After all, this world is passing away. Don't you want to put your time into something or someone that will have a lasting impact?

So, think back to that money you have, whatever the amount may be. What are you going to do with it?

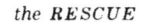

the **RESCUE**

WEEK THIRTY-SIX

DAY 2

"I am only one, but still I am one. I cannot do everything, but still I can do something; and because I cannot do everything, I will not refuse to do something that I can do." – Edward Everett Hale, *Bartlett's Familiar Quotations*

Movie plots abound with superheroes determined to save the world. Marvel has Captain America, Spider-Man, Iron Man, Black Widow, and others. DC has Batman, Superman, Flash, Wonder Woman, and more. But as inspirational as some of these characters may be, one person alone can't save the world. The good news is that Jesus has already defeated sin and death to do just that.

God is not asking you to be a superhero. He is asking for you to be obedient. Don't let the fact that you cannot do everything and save everyone keep you from pouring your time and energy into doing the one thing that God desires of you to make a difference.

the RESCUE

WEEK THIRTY-SIX
DAY 3

"Each one must give as he has decided in his heart, not reluctantly or under compulsion, for God loves a cheerful giver." - 2 Corinthians 9:7

Today, consider what you give to God and to others. If it helps, take a moment and jot down the ways in which you give.

You might see that God is really blessing others through your unselfishness. But, what you might find is that the list may turn out to be rather small.

Once you've evaluated your giving practices, take a moment and really search your heart to determine if you are a "cheerful giver." If not, spend some time in prayer asking God to give you the desire to give more and to give freely. Trust that He will do just that.

WEEK 37

the RESCUE

the **RESCUE**

WEEK 37
DAY 1

"Do not be anxious about anything, but in everything by prayer and supplication with thanksgiving let your requests be made known to God." - Philippians 4:6

Have you seen those athletic shirts with Philippians 4:13 ("I can do all things through Christ . . .") printed on them? The intent of the shirt is noble, namely that we can work hard and do hard things through the strength Christ gives us. While the intent may be in the right place, Paul certainly didn't mean that if we try hard enough we can run a sub-four-minute mile.

Read Philippians 4:6 and continue on through verse 13. Paul wrote this letter to the church at Philippi while he was in prison. Prison wasn't even the worst of Paul's harsh circumstances. (Just check out 2 Cor. 11:24-28.) Yet, he not only tells the church not to be anxious but also to straight up rejoice! Paul didn't intend for this kind of rejoicing to be based on circumstances, obviously, as he experienced all kinds of good and bad circumstances. Rather, it was based on an inner trust and reliance upon God. Because of his trust in God, Paul boldly prayed to God and asked Him for intervention. No matter how God answered, though, Paul could rejoice because He knew and trusted God.

Paul's statement that he could do anything in Christ's strength was rooted in the context of difficult life circumstances. But, the strength to seek God's Kingdom in any circumstance came from Christ. When we bring our worries before God, He may answer differently than we want, but when we trust Him, we can confidently trust and say, "I can do all things through Christ who gives me strength."

Consider This . . .
· What does it say about ourselves and our view of God when we think we know better than God does?

· Letting go of worry doesn't mean that life won't be painful at times. How can we deepen our relationship with God so that we can still rejoice in "all things"?

the RESCUE

WEEK 37 DAY 2

When we have lots of overwhelming circumstances (or just one overwhelming situation), sometimes it's hard to see anything positive if we aren't looking for it. As you go through your week, specifically look for ways that God has shown His care for you and opportunities you have to serve Him as your King. Or, you can also look back at pictures on your phone or your parents' phones to see how God's hand has been evident in your life, even in the midst of worrisome circumstances.

God is Father.
How have you seen Him care for you?

God is King.
What opportunities do you have to live in His way, according to His Word?

the **RESCUE**

WEEK 37 DAY 3

Sometimes people close to us do things that rightly cause us to lose trust in them. Sometimes things that have happened in our lives unjustly cause us to lose trust in God when we don't maintain an eternal and/or a Kingdom perspective.

In the space below, confess some of your doubts about God to Him.

Then, write a prayer asking for forgiveness and the strength to trust Him in all circumstances.

Finally, write a prayer thanking Him for His good, trustworthy, and sovereign character.

the RESCUE

WEEK

38
the RESCUE

the RESCUE

WEEK 38 DAY 1

"But God shows his love for us in that while we were still sinners, Christ died for us." - Romans 5:8

One of the reasons it's so easy for us to judge others is that people are messed up! Right? When we get frustrated with our own lives and start looking around with a worldly attitude, people's flaws become blaringly obvious. Have you ever fallen into this habit?

If you think about the people that frustrate you the most and multiply that by the number of people that have existed – ever – you begin to get an idea of how big the concept of sin really is. Every deed that falls short of holiness is an insult to God. Not only does He have the right to judge because He is Creator, but because ultimately He is the one being wronged.

But in His judgment there is MERCY!

Read Romans 5:6-8 and mark it in your Bible.

God doesn't engage in the same kind of bitterness that takes root in our hearts when we judge others. He judges in love. His judgment is perfect because all His ways are perfect. Even when we were guilty, He offers us forgiveness. God sacrificed Himself for us while we were still against Him.

Consider This . . .
· What does this reveal about God's character?

· How do we show the loving character of God when we refrain from judging others?

· Take a moment and meet God in prayer, asking God to help you see others today in a way that reflects His love.

WEEK 38 DAY 2

"Finally, brothers, whatever is true, whatever is honorable, whatever is just, whatever is pure, whatever is lovely, whatever is commendable, if there is any excellence, if there is anything worthy of praise, think about these things." - Philippians 4:8

One of the best ways to refocus our hearts and protect ourselves from becoming bitter and judgmental is to choose to see beyond the surface. This is what Christ does for us. Even though we are all sinful, we are all still image bearers of God. When you look at a person who is far from God, you either choose to see an opportunity to cast judgment, or an opportunity to glorify God by sharing forgiveness. When you see the faults in another Christ-follower, you can see failure or God's patience in our sanctification.

In every situation, we must make a choice with our mind in efforts to guide our hearts. Feelings and thoughts are closely related.

Consider This . . .
- Think of one person who you may have a tendency to judge. As you read Philippians 4:8, ask God to help you see how He is at work in that person's life. Take a moment in the space below to write down your prayer.

- Now, here is the challenge. Grab a piece of paper and write a note of encouragement to this person. Be careful that your words remain loving and uplifting. Maybe have a parent or close friend read it to make sure that it will be a positive influence. Pray for this person. And if you're feeling brave, deliver the note to them today.

the RESCUE

WEEK 38 DAY 3

"There is therefore now no condemnation for those who are in Christ Jesus."
- Romans 8:1

When we study what the Bible teaches about judging, we typically focus on our judgment of others. But many people struggle with judging themselves. Have you ever wrestled with feelings of guilt, depression, failure, insecurity, or any other internal conflict that keeps you from feeling like you can contribute to God's Kingdom? You are not alone in those feelings! The apostle Paul, who has a reputation as a pretty successful guy in the Kingdom of God, struggled with this too.

Read Romans 7:21-8:2

We are forgiven in Christ, but we still dwell in a sinful body. This is why we need to walk so closely to our Savior. Take a minute and think about some of your own shortcomings. How can God be glorified as He works through you despite your flaws? Instead of judging ourselves, God wants us to submit to Him and lay our failures at His feet. When we do this, we are ready to be used for His glory!

In the space below, make a two-column list of your strengths and weaknesses. Ask God to show you how He can use both of these columns to impact the world through you. Pray to God asking Him to help you let go and trust Him as He continues to work on you.

week 39

the RESCUE

the **RESCUE**

week 39 day 1

"But be doers of the word, and not hearers only, deceiving yourselves. For if anyone is a hearer of the word and not a doer, he is like a man who looks intently at his natural face in a mirror. For he looks at himself and goes away and at once forgets what he was like. But the one who looks into the perfect law, the law of liberty, and perseveres, being no hearer who forgets but a doer who acts, he will be blessed in his doing." - James 1:22-25

Think about the scenario that James talks about: when would you ever look at yourself in a mirror and forget what you looked like? That's crazy! You probably know exactly what you look like even without looking at a mirror - we look at ourselves a lot.

We're really good at knowing our own appearances, but we're not so great at remembering the things that God is calling us to do.

We read the Bible and then go and live however we want. James says that's the same thing as looking in a mirror, seeing that you have salad stuck in your teeth and then leaving and doing nothing about it!

As much as we deny it, that's exactly what we do with God's Word. When we read the Bible, God begins to show us things in our lives that don't match up. If we never do anything about those problems, not only are we not following God, we're forgetting what we saw in the mirror of our souls!

God calls us not only to read His Word, but to follow it. We're not just to be hearers, but doers. We're not called to follow so that God will notice us, but because He already has! Because Jesus died for us, we live for Him!

Consider This . . .

· What do you think James means in verse 22 when he says that people who are hearers only are "deceiving" themselves?

· What are some things that you feel like God has shown you about yourself through reading His Word? Is there anything you need to change or work on?

· Pray that God would help you remember and act. Ask God to help you not forget what you look like, and to give you the strength to look more like Him.

week 39 DAY 2

For the past few weeks, we've been looking at the Sermon on the Mount that Jesus gives to a large crowd of people. Daniel Doriani wrote this about Jesus' sermon:

"When we listen to the Sermon on the Mount, we do not simply hear Jesus' words. We hear Jesus" *(The Sermon on the Mount: The Character of a Disciple).*

Think about what he is saying there. When Jesus was preaching to this crowd of people on a mountaintop thousands of years ago, He wasn't just talking to them, He was talking to *you!*

Consider This . . .
- Jesus knew thousands of years ago that you would follow Him! He was praying for you, teaching you, and providing for you even then!

- What are some of the words of Jesus that you love to hear?

- What are some of the words of Jesus that are hard to follow?

- Spend some time praying that God will help you really listen to the words of Jesus. Pray that the words of Christ will begin to change your heart and make you more like Him.

the RESCUE

week 39 DAY 3

Take a second and read 2 Timothy 3:16.

In this verse, Paul writes that the Word of God is useful for several different things. Now, in the space provided, for each of the traits of God's Word, write out ways that God has done that in your life. If you don't feel like that's ever happened before, write out some ways that you think God might want that to happen in your heart.

TEACHING - How has God taught you from His Word?

REPROOF - Reproof is when we read God's Word and we realize that we've been doing something wrong. Has that ever happened?

CORRECTION - Has reading God's Word ever caused you to change your mind on something?

TRAINING IN RIGHTEOUSNESS - How has reading God's Word taught you how to live for Him? What may He be calling you to do?

Consider This . . .
- Spend some time in prayer thanking God for His Word. He has preserved it over thousands of years so that you could read it to know Him. Ask Him to continue teaching you from it forever!

the RESCUE

WEEK

FORTY

the RESCUE

WEEK FORTY DAY 1

"For what does it profit a man to gain the whole world and forfeit his soul? For what can a man give in return for his soul?" - Mark 8:36-37

Turn on the TV or scroll through social media and you'll see advertisements for just about anything. We are trained to want. More money. More comfort. A nicer phone. A better computer. We have rooms full of stuff and we still want more. We think we need more because it would make life better for us.

If we are honest, most of our decisions revolve around what we want, what feels the most comfortable, or what we think is best for us. We spend so much time trying to please ourselves and so little time thinking about what pleases God.

Read Mark 8:36-37. Jesus asks the question, "What does it profit a man to gain the whole world and forfeit his soul?" What good is it to have the best of everything in this life if you will spend an eternity separated from God?

Rather than seeking to gain all the riches and pleasures of this world, we should seek to walk closely with Jesus and remove anything from our lives that prevent us from complete obedience. Any self-denial or suffering that we face for the sake of Christ, and for the Gospel, will be worth it all when we spend an eternity with our mighty Rescuer, Christ Jesus.

Those who have been rescued by Christ are called to be different. We are called to deny ourselves. We're called to face suffering in this world in order to gain the riches of eternity with Christ in heaven. Rather than training ourselves to want what the world has to offer, we should train ourselves to want the riches that only a relationship with Christ can offer.

Consider This . . .
- What in my life is keeping me from following Christ in a more committed way?

the **RESCUE**

WEEK FORTY

DAY 2

Take some time this week and look for actions of self-denial in others.

Maybe you will notice one of your parents giving up their time to serve you or one of your siblings. Maybe you'll notice a teacher spending extra time helping another student in need. Perhaps you'll see a friend sharing his or her lunch money so that someone else doesn't go hungry. Perhaps you know someone who gets up extra early to spend time in God's Word.

Ready for an extra challenge? When you see an act of self-denial in service to another, encourage that person. You can send a text, write a short note, or just say a kind word.

Think about how denying self to serve others is one way to follow Jesus more closely.

the RESCUE

WEEK *FORTY*
DAY 3

In Mark 8:34, Jesus said, "If anyone would come after me, let him deny himself..."

Consider This . . .
· Do you think most people deny themselves? Or are most people self-centered and focused on the things of this world?

· What makes you say that?

· How about you? Do you put aside your desires and interests to have a deeper relationship with Christ? Or do you prefer to do what makes you happy?

· Do you spend more time thinking about yourself and the things of this world, or about bringing God glory?

· Spend a moment in prayer today talking to God about what it practically looks like for you to deny yourself.

WEEK 41
the RESCUE

the RESCUE

WEEK 41
DAY 1

This week you wrote a letter asking the Lord to help you be "clothed" in His attributes. Take that letter out now, or think about what you wrote.

Read the passage we reflected on again:

"Therefore, as God's chosen people, holy and dearly loved, clothe yourselves with compassion, kindness, humility, gentleness and patience. Bear with each other and forgive one another if any of you has a grievance against someone. Forgive as the Lord forgave you. And over all these virtues put on love, which binds them all together in perfect unity." – Colossians 3:12-14

Now look back at your letter or what you wrote. Next, notice that the only "attribute" that covers that rest is love. This is the love of Christ and it covers everything and all of us. We can't be clothed with anything if we aren't covered by His love. As we draw close to Christ and learn how to live out our lives with Him, He is the one that helps us wear these clothes of godly attributes. We can't put on any of this without a relationship with Him.

Consider This . . .
· What is it you asked the Lord to help you with this week? Ask Him to clothe you with HIs love and show you what that means.

· Are there some people that you don't want forgive? Why? Ask God what it means to forgive them with His forgiveness.

the **RESCUE**

WEEK 41 DAY 2

Find the heaviest and most comfortable coat or sweatshirt you own and put it on right now, as you do this devotion.

Feel its weight and warmth. Imagine this is what it feels like to be totally clothed with Christ's love.

If you lived like Christ's love covered you totally like this coat or sweatshirt, how would you live differently?

Ask the Lord in prayer to show you what it means to walk a life clothed in His love. Use the space below to write this prayer if you choose:

the RESCUE

WEEK 41 DAY 3

Today take a few moments to ask God about one person you have a hard time getting along with or forgiving. Use the space below if you choose:

Tell Him the truth about what you feel about this person and why.

Get it all out in total honesty with the Lord. Then ask Him to show you what forgiving this person would mean.

the RESCUE

WEEK 42
the RESCUE

the **RESCUE**

WEEK 42 DAY 1

"Rejoice always, pray continually, give thanks in all circumstances; for this is God's will for you in Christ Jesus." - 1 Thessalonians 5:16-18

Back in 1908 most cars that were being produced were too expensive for the average American to own. Automobiles were mostly custom made involving much time and human labor. Henry Ford's Model T was the first car to be mass-produced on an assembly line, which brought the price way down. By the time production ended in 1927 some 15 million Model T's had been manufactured by Ford, and in 1999 it was named the most influential car of the 20th century.

You don't see many Model T Fords on the road today. While the styles of cars have changed, the basic idea of assembly line production created by Henry Ford continues to be the standard for automobile manufacturing. The Lord's Prayer you learned about in this week's Bible study may be 2,000 years old, but the idea of models in prayer are still effective today. Other Bible writers like the apostle Paul added new dimensions to prayer like rejoicing, praying always, and being thankful. The scriptures are full of these models to help you have a dynamic prayer life.

Consider This . . .
· Take some time to look at other models of prayer in the Bible like Philippians 4:6-7, 1 John 5:14, and Colossians 4:2.

· What are some of the parts of your model prayers each day?

· What would it be like to model your prayers off of Scripture? Why or why not? Do you think it would be helpful if you did?

WEEK 42 DAY 2

"True prayer is measured by weight, not by length. A single groan before God may have more fullness of prayer in it than a fine oration of great length."
- C. H. Spurgeon

"In prayer it is better to have a heart without words than words without a heart."
- John Bunyan

"Prayer is not learned in a classroom but in the closet." - E. M. Bounds

"Prayer does not fit us for the greater work; prayer is the greater work."
- Oswald Chambers

These are four great quotes on prayer from some awesome men of God. Take some time to read these quotes and think about what is being said be these men. Think about ways these quotes could change your thinking and your approach to prayer. Pick one of the quotes and write it down on a piece of paper and place it somewhere that you can see it every day for the next week.

Let the words of these giants for God help you in your personal prayer life.

the RESCUE

WEEK 42 DAY 3

Get your cell phone and set the alarm to go off in 15 minutes.

Get someplace where you can be alone and turn off all the distractions like your TV, computer, etc.

Now, spend the next 15 minutes doing nothing but praying to God and thinking about Him. You may want to use The Lord's Prayer as a guide, as you spend your quiet time alone with God. Let's get started.

When you're done, consider this . . .
· What about it was difficult? What about it was easy?

· Did you feel God speak to you?

· How did it feel to be faithful to what Jesus called you to do in prayer?

· So when will you schedule your next 15 minute encounter with God?

week 43

the RESCUE

the RESCUE

week 43 day 1

"Blessed is the man who walks not in the counsel of the wicked, nor stands in the way of sinners, nor sits in the seat of scoffers." - Psalm 1:1

Compromise. It is one thing that takes people down and ruins their character. Whether it is a famous person or a teenager, a slip into compromise can ruin you and your witness for Jesus to a watching world.

The first verse of the Book of Psalms speaks of compromises that so many people have fallen into. We listen to and take advice from the wicked. We stand in and act in the ways of sinners. We sit down with scoffers.

Have you ever been there? You might not think it's a big deal. You don't think that you'll make the bad decision. You're just hanging around it, not actually doing it. But while checking it out, you slowly become more and more comfortable with the sin that is in front of you. You begin to slip down a very slippery slope.

The slippery slope eventually ends with us sitting. We are now part of the group. We find ourselves participating in the evil decisions. We have slowly and subtly slipped into compromise. We wake up one day and realize that the evil we first walked by is now the evil in which we live and make our decisions.

Are you slipping? Do you have someone in your life that will help pull you out if you are on the slope and don't realize it?

Consider This . . .
- Where are you when it comes to evil decisions and compromise?

- What desire are you trying to fulfill as you slip toward sin and compromise? How can you look to Jesus instead?

- Ask people around you to call you out when they see you beginning to slip.

week 43 DAY 2

In the space provided, spend some time today writing a letter to Jesus. Look back at your notecard from the lesson. Talk to Him about the things that you tend to value and treasure more than Him.

Ask Him to reveal to you what you're seeking in those things. Ask Him to reveal to you how He is the One that truly meets our deepest desires and longings. Talk to Him about your desire for Him continuing to grow.

the RESCUE

week 43 | DAY 3

Today, do something different. Put down your phone. Turn off the video game. Do whatever you need to do to get by yourself and get alone with God. Outside.

Get outside, go for a walk, and have a conversation with Jesus. Imagine that He is there walking beside you. Spend some time sharing about your desire to know Him more.

Most importantly, listen to what He has to say to you.

WEEK

FORTY-FOUR

the RESCUE

WEEK *FORTY-FOUR* DAY 1

"And being found in human form, he humbled himself by becoming obedient to the point of death, even death on a cross." - Philippians 2:8

When we think of being humble, we usually think of it in terms of not bragging too much about ourselves. But pride is so much more than that. In short, pride says, "Me first." If you're honest, you can probably think of a few places in your life where you tend to be "me first" instead of "others first."

Read Philippians 2:3-8. Paul was writing to Christians in Philippi who were experiencing persecution—pressure from outside their church from people who wanted them to stop worshipping only Jesus. That pressure had begun to cause some conflict within their church. That added stress made them start to look more to their own interests, rather than the interests of others.

So Paul uses the example of Jesus to show them what the opposite of "me first" is. Jesus gave Himself away by dying on the cross so that we could life forever. And by using Jesus as an example, the implication is pretty clear: the way we follow Jesus is by giving ourselves away as well.

Consider This . . .
· Why is it so hard to treat others as though they are more significant or important than we are?

· Think of one person who has done this for you; one person who had looked to your interests before their own. How does it feel when someone does that for you?

· Think back to the Bible study from this week—everyone identified one specific goal for using a gift God has given us to serve others. How's it going?

the **RESCUE**

WEEK FORTY-FOUR

DAY 2

This week we talked about how God gives us gifts—both possessions and talents we might have—in order to serve others.

But sometimes we aren't really sure we have much that we can use to serve others. So today you've got a pretty simple task that might actually be harder than it sounds . . .

In the space provided, write down 10 gifts that God has given you, whether it's a possession or a talent you have. Yep, 10. Do it now.

1.
2.
3.
4.
5.
6.
7.
8.
9.
10.

Now, take a minute and thank God for each of those gifts by name. Listen for what God might tell you about using these gifts to serve others.

WEEK FORTY-FOUR
DAY 3

Take a second and read this quote:

"The value of a life is measured in terms of how much of it was given away."
– Andy Stanley

That's a much different way of looking at the "good life" than we're used to, isn't it?

Consider This . . .
· Do you think the quote is true? Why or why not?

· Who is someone you admire for serving others so much you could say they give their life away?

· What is one way you could give your life away more than you do now?

Spend some time praying for God to work on your heart so that your desire is to "give your life away."

WEEK 45
the RESCUE

the **RESCUE**

WEEK 45
DAY 1

"For by grace you have been saved through faith. And this is not your own doing; it is the gift of God, not a result of works, so that no one may boast."
- Ephesians 2:8-9

You've probably heard the old adage, "You get what you pay for." The idea is if you get something cheap, then chances are it's not a great product. For instance, if you purchase a small plastic spinning top for a quarter out of the machine by the exit of your favorite "all you can eat" buffet, you're not going to expect it to be the greatest toy of all time. Why? Because you typically get what you pay for.

Read Ephesians 2:8-9. Wow! According to this passage, when it comes to salvation we get what we didn't pay for. We can't earn being saved. We can't pay for it. We don't deserve it. God saved us from sin and death by His grace. Grace is God's unmerited favor, which means underserved or unearned kindness. In other words, salvation is a free gift given by God to those who believe. We don't pay a dime, yet we get the best of the best.

How is this possible? As the hymn says, "Jesus paid it all." He paid the full price for our salvation when He laid down His life for us on the cross. He purchased our salvation with His own blood. By grace, He then offers it to us as a gift. You see Christians get what Jesus paid for. That's grace.

Consider This . . .
· How does it make you feel to know that salvation is a gift?

· Why is it important to remember that salvation cost Jesus so much?

· Is this a message that would be worth sharing today? Who do you know how might need to hear that salvation is a free gift?

WEEK 45 DAY 2

Take a moment and read this quote:

"From the start, God's simple design has been for every single disciple of Jesus to make disciples who make disciples who make disciples until the Gospel spreads to all peoples on the planet." - Robby Gallaty, *Growing Up: How to Be A Disciple Who Makes Disciples*

God's plan is for personal discipleship to make a global impact.

Consider This . . .
· Why is following God's simple plan for multiplication so difficult to practice?

· What obstacles are preventing you from being a disciple who makes disciples?

· Have you ever thought that you could have a small part in the gospel spreading to the entire world? How does that make you feel?

Spend some time in prayer with the Lord, asking Him to reveal to you how He desires to use you to make the Gospel known to the nations.

the **RESCUE**

WEEK 45 DAY 3

Today, write a letter to one person in your life who needs to hear the good news that Jesus rescues sinners like you and me.

We've talked about sharing the Gospel with others this week, and perhaps you haven't had an opportunity to share yet. This is your chance. You don't have to give it to the person (although you may want to). It will be a great way for you to think through how you would share with someone so you'll be prepared. Who knows, God might lead you to give the person a copy of the letter or give you the opportunity to share with him or her in person.

WEEK 46
the RESCUE

the **RESCUE**

WEEK 46 DAY 1

"Great is the LORD, and greatly to be praised, and his greatness is unsearchable." - Psalm 145:3

God is great. You most likely knew this. - But check out the rest of Psalm 145:3. Not only is God great, He is greatly to be praised. What does this mean? It means that God is uniquely worthy of your praise. He alone deserves your full praise and worship.

So, today, let's do something that may be a little different. Spend some time thinking about the greatness of God. Spend time thinking about how He has showed Himself great in your personal life, and throughout creation. Then, spend some time audibly praising the Lord.

That's right. Audibly. Out loud. You can simply tell God how awesome He is, or you can sing to Him. The important part is to make time to praise Him one on one.

When you're finished, use the space provided to write down how this made you feel. Then, take some time in the next few days to do this again.

WEEK 46
DAY 2

At the heart of praise, is appreciation and gratitude.

So, today, spend some time cultivating an attitude of gratitude for the Lord and all that He has done for you by remembering His past and present blessings in your life.

Let's do something cool. In the space below, write out as many blessings as you can think of. The challenge is to think of 100 blessings. Can you do it?

When you're done, spend a moment in prayer thanking God for all His blessings.

the **RESCUE**

WEEK 46 DAY 3

Check out this quote:

> "MISSIONS IS NOT THE ULTIMATE GOAL OF THE CHURCH. WORSHIP IS. MISSIONS EXISTS BECAUSE WORSHIP DOESN'T. WORSHIP IS ULTIMATE, NOT MISSIONS, BECAUSE GOD IS ULTIMATE, NOT MAN. WHEN THIS AGE IS OVER, AND THE COUNTLESS MILLIONS OF THE REDEEMED FALL ON THEIR FACES BEFORE THE THRONE OF GOD, MISSIONS WILL BE NO MORE."

–JOHN PIPER, LET THE NATIONS BE GLAD! THE SUPREMACY OF GOD IN MISSIONS.

We are often encouraged, as we should be, to share our faith with others. If we are not careful though, we can think this is the ultimate purpose of our salvation. Missions is extremely important, but evangelism is second to worshiping God ourselves. In fact, if we fail to regularly and whole-heartedly worship God, we will not make great witnesses for Him. We cannot speak much of a God we have not fully experienced. We cannot give water from a well we have let run dry.

Commit to creating practical patterns of worship in your life. If you are unsure how to do this, then ask your youth minister, Bible study teacher, or Christian relative or friend to teach you.

week 47

the RESCUE

the RESCUE

week **47** *day* **1**

"Do not conform to the pattern of this world, but be transformed by the renewing of your mind. Then you will be able to test and approve what God's will is—his good, pleasing and perfect will." - Romans 12:2

In 2012, the snack company Hostess began the process to shut its doors forever. One of its most popular snack cakes was the Twinkie, and people began to lose their minds that Twinkies would become a thing of the past. Taking advantage of their desperation, boxes began appearing on eBay. Desperate, some people paid $60 or more for a box—over 10 times what the box would cost in a store. Fear, greed, and the unknown set up a subjective value on these snack cakes.

Read Romans 12:2.

Paul instructed his readers to be transformed into the likeness of Christ by rejecting the things of this world and being transformed through the work of the Spirit within them to renew their minds. This transformation was not something that his readers could do themselves. Rather, it is the work of the Lord through the Spirit to bring their way of thinking more and more in line with God's ways.

However, we must recognize that believers are still sinful, and our transformation is a lifelong process. We cannot, then, place our own thoughts on the same level of authority as God's unchanging Word. Read 2 Timothy 3:16-17. God has given us His Word so that we can have an objective measure we can use to know God and His will. Without a way to test our own thoughts and experiences, we are at risk of drifting away from God's standards and will. Like those Twinkies fans, we can let emotions and sinful hearts drive us to make costly decisions. Although we can have confidence in the Spirit's active work in our lives as believers, we cannot overestimate our propensity for sin; we must look to God's Word to guide us.

Consider This . . .

· Why is it so dangerous to not check our experiences and thoughts with what God tells us in His Word?

· How can God's Word give us confidence in knowing His will and then following through?

week 47 DAY 2

This week's lesson discussed the influential nature of the Gospel in our lives and how it is to impact everything we do. From the way we study to the purpose in our lives, everything is to reflect the saving power of the Gospel that has redeemed us. Living this way is different than just being "a good person" according to our culture. Living in light of the Gospel means that we make a conscious choice to follow the commands and will of God, as He has given us in His Word.

Sometimes, living as people who have been redeemed is in contrast to what our cultures deems as "good." Increasingly, our culture believes that one's religious beliefs are to be kept to oneself and put in a little box, only to be opened and explored personally.

As you talk with friends, interact on social media, and observe news stories this week, keep an eye out for cultural challenges to living according to God's Word. When you see these challenges, how do they make you feel? When you feel uncomfortable or pressured, how can you have confidence in God's Word and in the Gospel to stand strong?

Also, keep an eye out for posts or stories of encouragement about following Christ. How can you encourage others who are experiencing challenges to live fully by the truth of the Gospel?

week 47 DAY 3

Believers are told in Romans 12:2 to not conform to the ways of the world.

Consider the definition of the word "conform" to mean "fashioning out of the same pattern" or "molded to the same form." What images come to mind when you read this definition? Being one in a row of dresses that all look alike? Being a cookie cutter version of everyone else? Being boxed up in a row of identical action figures? All of these images give a good word picture of conforming to something.

Sometimes the idea of conforming sets us on a rebellion because the world encourages us to be unique, and being unique is pretty great sometimes. But, there are times when conforming is good. For instance, when you are taught that 2+2=4, it's good to acknowledge that there are rules of mathematics. Can you think of other times when conforming is good?

What about when we are conforming to all that God has designed us to be? What if, when we are conforming to God's Word, we are becoming the best person we could be?

So, what are you conforming to? A cookie cutter image of the world? Or becoming the unique, God-designed, individual He created you to be?

If you need some guidance as you consider what you are conforming to, look up Galatians 5:22-24. There's a list of characteristics in those verses that describe someone who is conforming to the image of Christ.

WEEK FORTY-EIGHT

the RESCUE

WEEK *FORTY-EIGHT* DAY 1

"But all these things they will do to you on account of my name, because they do not know him who sent me." - John 15:21

Can you think of a controversial topic that is the subject of public debate right now? The sad truth is, it may be harder to think of just one at a time! Every single day we see heated issues like politics, education, religious freedom, gender identity, sanctity of life, and even the idea of morality debated by thousands in the public eye. Social media adds to this epidemic with everyone firing off their views, often with little-to-no information or contemplation. What's the bottom line? It is not as popular as it once was to be a Christian in America!

Re-read the passage from this week's lesson: John 15:18-21.

Consider This ...
- How does today's social climate prove this passage to be true?

- How can Christ-followers view this public hatred as an opportunity for the Gospel to be shared?

- Does the shift in public opinion make you feel differently about your faith? How so?

the RESCUE

WEEK FORTY-EIGHT

DAY 2

A few years ago it seemed like the biggest worldview issue young believers had to deal with was the presentation of evolution and the Big Bang Theory that seemed to contradict Creation. Many of the people who believe this are skeptical, and maybe even fearful, of the idea of an all-powerful creator.

But, the issues are quickly getting more complicated.

Take a few minutes and flip through the news headlines or scroll through your newsfeed on social media. Do you see evidence of society being anti-Christian? You really don't have to look very hard to find it. Choose a particular issue and ask yourself these questions:

· How does this particular issue reflect hatred or opposition toward Christianity?

· How does this view reveal a lack of understanding of who God really is?

· How would a right understanding of God's nature and character change this view and reveal the truth about the situation?

Ask God to help you see current events the way He does and to make you a voice of Truth in your circle of influence.

the RESCUE

WEEK *FORTY-EIGHT*
DAY 3

Read 1 Corinthians 13.

You may have heard these verses read if you have attended a wedding, but these words are not really just about marriage. In fact, Paul was speaking to the church at Corinth as they dealt with social issues that were leading them into sin. Many of them were still trying to be like the unbelievers around them. Just like our passage in John 15 reminds us that we do not belong to the world, Paul had to remind these believers that they belonged to God.

Only God has ownership over our lives. This means that our thoughts, emotions, and actions should be rooted in who He is and what we stand for in Him.

Read over 1 Corinthians again and underline the words that describe what real love looks like.

- Write a couple of your favorite phrases that describe God-honoring love.

- Is it possible to have the "right" answer to a person or problem and communicate it in a way that does not bring honor to God? In what way?

- What does this passage say we are like if we confront the world with truth WITHOUT love?

When you seek to confront the culture that is against the Truth, you have to remember who you are and WHOSE you are. We represent our God when we speak His truth. Show His love!

WEEK 49

the RESCUE

the RESCUE

WEEK 49
DAY 1

"Count it all joy, my brothers, when you meet trials of various kinds, for you know that the testing of your faith produces steadfastness. And let steadfastness have its full effect, that you may be perfect and complete, lacking in nothing."- James 1:2-4

Think about the last time you felt truly joyful. Was it when you went to the beach last summer? Could it be the best birthday you've had? Or when you finally got a good grade in that class you've been struggling with?

Usually, we associate joy with success. When things are going well for us, we feel happy! But James tells us something different in his letter. He says that we should be joyful even when we're struggling. James says that in the midst of our trials, we should have joy. Why?

We should be joyful because we know this: God is producing steadfastness in us. Literally, through trials, God is helping us become more faithful. When any particular trial is over, we come out more dependent on God. We trust God more! We trust Him because we know that He has been beside us through the hardest times.

It may seem hard to believe that we trust God more when we struggle, because we feel like God should help things go easy for us. After all, we are serving Him, right? God doesn't promise us an easy road and no difficulty, but He does promise to be with us every step of the way.

Consider This . . .
· What are some trials that you have faced in your life? Think about some times you have struggled in school, with your fiends, or with family. How has God helped you through those times? Reflecting on how God has helped us in the past helps us trust Him for tomorrow.

· Spend some time in prayer with God. Thank Him for how he has provided for you in the past and helped you through hard times. Take some deep breaths and realize the amazing truth that the God of the Universe wants to be with you. He is beside His children, every step of the way.

the **RESCUE**

WEEK 49 DAY 2

This week we talked about suffering. In Scripture, the Apostle Paul was a guy who knew suffering well. While preaching the Gospel he was shipwrecked, beaten, imprisoned, and was even bitten by a snake once (see Acts 28 for that crazy story)! Can you imagine that many things going wrong while you were trying to serve Jesus? Don't you think it would be hard to keep on serving God with that many things going wrong? Listen to what he told his friend Timothy:

"If we are faithless, He remains faithful." - 2 Timothy 2:13

In that simple phrase, Paul lets us in on a secret: he did find it hard to keep serving sometimes! But the key to Paul's desire to keep serving was this: he knew that Jesus wasn't going to give up on him! Paul knew that Jesus would always be faithful.

Consider This . . .
· Has something ever gone wrong in your life when you were trying to serve God? How did that make you feel? Do you ever feel like God can't see you?

· Read Paul's quote again. Isn't it encouraging to know that even when we lose perspective on who God is, He always remains faithful? God will never change who He is!

· Spend some time praying that God will help you to be faithful like He is faithful. Ask God to help you stay committed to Him even when it's hard.

the RESCUE

WEEK 49 DAY 3

Check this out: the average lifespan of an American is about 79 years.

Think about that. Hopefully, you've got a lot more life yet to live! In a journal or a drawing app, draw one square for every five years you've been alive. Draw a line for every single year. (So, 16 years old would be three squares and 1 line.)

Think about all that has happened in your life in just that short amount of time!

Write out some of the best things that have happened in that time:

Now, write out some of the biggest struggles you've had.

Now, think about all the blocks you'd have to draw if you drew blocks that represented the rest of your life. There will be some good times and some difficult times in those empty blocks. There will be some times where it's easy to follow God and some times where you won't feel like following God at all. As we've been talking about, life as a citizen of the Kingdom of God, we have to realize that, even when it's hard, the best thing we can do is follow God. If we ever doubt His love for us, we only have to remember the cross: He died for us.

Consider This . . .
Spend some time in prayer thanking God for all the ways He has provided for you. (Write it out if it helps.) Ask Him to help you remember His love for you even in the future, when things may get hard!

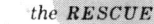

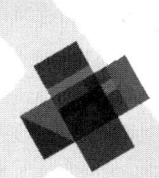

the RESCUE

WEEK 50
the RESCUE

the RESCUE

WEEK 50 DAY 1

"And do not fear those who kill the body but cannot kill the soul. Rather fear him who can destroy both soul and body in hell." - Matthew 10:28

Have you ever been to the zoo? Looking at the lions, tigers, or bears can instantly strike terror in your heart and make you thankful that there is a barrier between you and an animal that has the power to end your life. We recognize that the power of the animal is greater than our power, and the proper response is a respectful fear. This is good and healthy because it guides us to act with wisdom.

There are good fears and bad fears. Jesus speaks of both. Read Matthew 10:28.

Jesus tells us that we should not fear those who can physically harm us. We cannot let the fear of suffering keep us from taking a stand for Christ. Those who kill the body have limited power. No matter what they do to us, they cannot take away our salvation. There is nothing they can do to separate us from the love of God in Christ.

To fear mere humans is to care more about what others think than what God thinks. To fear humans is to let the words and actions of others determine how we behave. The fear of others is a bad fear because it considers the power of people greater than the power of God. It will keep us from obeying Him.

Jesus says that instead of fearing these humans with limited power, we should fear God, who is all-powerful. The fear of God is a good fear because we recognize that God has power over every person and circumstance. It helps us to trust Him no matter what comes our way.

Consider This . . .
· You will fear that which you believe has the most power. That fear will guide your thoughts and actions. Will you choose to fear God or fear men?

· How does this impact the way you pursue your faith?

WEEK 50
DAY 2

Take a moment and read this quote:

"If we knew the depths of our sin and the heights of God's love for us, we'd never have to be afraid of anything." - Marshall Segal

Then, think about the following questions:

- Jesus tells us, "Do not fear." How can knowing the depths of our sin and the heights of God's love for us help us to obey Jesus' command?

- How can thinking about the death, burial, and resurrection of Christ erase our fears?

WEEK 50 DAY 3

Today, take a few minutes to watch some birds.

Seriously.

As you watch them fly, perch, chirp, look for food, or build a nest, think about God's knowledge and care over them.

Remember that Jesus says you are of more value to God than the birds.

Take time today to praise God for His sovereign care over you. Record your thoughts in the space provided if it helps.

week 51

the RESCUE

the RESCUE

week 51 day 1

"So we do not lose heart. Though our outer self is wasting away, our inner self is being renewed day by day. For this light momentary affliction is preparing for us an eternal weight of glory beyond all comparison, as we look not to the things that are seen but to the things that are unseen. For the things that are seen are transient, but the things that are unseen are eternal." - 2 Corinthians 4:16-18

Trials are difficult; there is no doubt about that. We can ask God to take them away, and instead it can just feel like life simply gets harder. God may seem distant, and nothing changes no matter how hard you pray. Yet, God gives us a promise in these times.

Notice the first phrase in this passage: "Do not lose heart." In other words, even though life "feels" difficult, God wants to remind us that He is close. He has not forgotten us. The choice lies in where we allow our mind to dwell. We can spend all of our time thinking about the circumstances, how we don't like them and want them to change. If they don't change, however, and this is all we think about, chances are we will start to grow angry, bitter, or at the very least, hopeless. So, we have to take the time and choose to "fix our eyes" not on what we can see in the trials, but in the hope that is Christ. We have to look to Him to remember exactly what it means that we are not left alone.

Consider This . . .

· How are you feeling in the midst of whatever trial you are going through right now? Why?

· What can you do to take your focus off of things that don't go your way and instead get closer to Jesus? Will this help change things? Why?

week 51 DAY 2

Take out the paper you wrote on at the end of the lesson. Read over what you wrote. How is this situation going this week?

Now, add the words of 2 Corinthians 4:8-9 to it: "We are afflicted in every way, but not crushed; perplexed, but not driven to despair; persecuted, but not forsaken; struck down, but not destroyed." Put this somewhere you can see it this week.

The things you are going through may not be "over," but you can be reminded that God is with you in the middle of it all. Ask yourself: how can I point others to Christ through this situation?

the RESCUE

week 51 DAY 3

"A man can no more diminish God's glory by refusing to worship Him than a lunatic can put out the sun by scribbling the word 'darkness' on the walls of his cell." - C.S. Lewis

Today, as you think about where God is in the difficult times, take a moment to reflect on this quote.

God is still there whether or not you can "see" Him right now.

In the space provided below, write down your thoughts about this quote:

WEEK

FIFTY-TWO

the RESCUE

the **RESCUE**

WEEK *FIFTY-TWO* DAY 1

"And immediately he proclaimed Jesus in the synagogues, saying, "He is the Son of God." And all who heard him were amazed and said, "Is not this the man who made havoc in Jerusalem of those who called upon this name? And has he not come here for this purpose, to bring them bound before the chief priests?" But Saul increased all the more in strength, and confounded the Jews who lived in Damascus by proving that Jesus was the Christ." - Acts 9:20-22

Saul was a devout Jew who considered the killing of Christians a necessary part of his belief system. He was miraculously rescued from his old way of life when a brilliant light struck him blind on the road to Damascus. Saul discovered that Jesus was the Son of God, and his life was forever changed.

Notice what Saul, who would soon have his name changed to Paul, did very soon after his experience of spiritual rescue. The passage says that he immediately started preaching and proclaiming that Jesus is the Son of God. Your last lesson in The Rescue series was titled "Not Just Rescued FROM, But Rescued TO." Just like Saul, you have been rescued from sin and separation from God through Jesus Christ. Now it is time to get to the "Rescued TO" part.

Consider This . . .
· Why do you think Paul was so quick to begin proclaiming the good news of the Gospel?

· What are some things the Bible says a rescued person should do?

· Are you living life like someone who has been rescued to something amazing and wonderful?

Pray this week that God will help you live out loud your rescued life in Him.

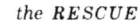

the **RESCUE**

WEEK FIFTY-TWO

DAY 2

This will be a devotion of meditation. Use a phone, tablet, or computer to look up the song Rescue by the group NewSong. Use your devotion time today to listen to this great song. Reflect on what this song says to you personally. Also, think of The Rescue Bible Study series you just finished and think back on key points that have stuck with you over the past year.

After listening to and meditating on the song, consider downloading it to listen to over the next week and let God continue to burn the message of rescue deep within your soul.

the **RESCUE**

WEEK FIFTY-TWO
DAY 3

This is your final devotion in The Rescue series. Hopefully you've had the opportunity to hear most of the lessons and spend time with most of the devotions. Take a few minutes and maybe find somewhere comfortable to sit or go on a walk and think about all you've learned during this series.

Consider This . . .

· Is there a particular lesson that you remember? What did you learn from it? What stood out to you?

· Is there a certain idea or theme that has stuck with you during this series? What is it? How has it impacted you?

· Is there a certain devotion that really spoke to you? What was memorable about it?

· Looking forward, how can you take what you've learned throughout the series and live a full, abundant life that points to Christ, our great Rescuer?

CLOSING

You've come to the end of the book. That's pretty awesome. Hopefully by this point you've grown in your understanding of God and of yourself. (That's the cool thing that happens when you spend time with God.) But before you go, we wanted to leave you with one final word . . .

In his letter to the Colossians, Paul writes this: "And so, from the day we heard, we have not ceased to pray for you, asking that you may be filled with the knowledge of his will in all spiritual wisdom and understanding, so as to walk in a manner worthy of the Lord, fully pleasing to him, bearing fruit in every good work and increasing in the knowledge of God." - Colossians 1:9-10

We want these verses to serve as a challenge of sorts. They are short but they pack a real punch. In them, you can find a few concepts that you might embrace as goals for your spiritual life. Especially as someone who is now fully aware of how the Gospel has transformed you.

The first of these challenges is that you would engage with God through the Bible. Paul says his prayer for the Colossians is that they would be "filled with the knowledge of God's will," and that this knowledge would be a full, well-rounded knowledge. Shouldn't this be our prayer for ourselves?

The second challenge is that you would live out God's ways. Knowing the Bible isn't enough. We must live it out. Paul says our knowledge of God leads to a life that is pleasing to God, where we "bear fruit in every good work."

The third challenge is to live in such a way that the first two challenges are repeated over and over again in your life. Paul describes a process of growing in knowledge so that your life would be fruitful . . . so that you can in turn continue to grow in knowledge! How awesome is that?!

You know the change the Gospel has made in your life. Now, your challenge is to live your life in such a way that you are constantly seeking God and growing in your faith.

ACKNOW-
LEDGMENTS

At YM360, we love taking a team approach to creating Gospel-driven, life-changing resources like *The Rescue* Bible study and *The Rescue Interactive Journal*.

Andy Blanks
Publisher, Executive Editor

Mark Jenkins
Associate Editor

Laurel-Dawn Berryhill
Art Director

Jeremi Beam
Paige Townley
Copy Editors

Ben Birdsong
Andy Blanks
Kristy Bruce
Kathleen Bryan
Leneita Fix
Mark Jenkins
Kevin Johnson
Chelsea Kellum
Benjer McVeigh
Brandon Nichols
Jenny Riddle
Richard Parker
Authors

WHAT KEEPS YOU FROM BEING ALL THAT GOD HAS CALLED YOU TO BE?

Whatever it is, you need to know this: there is a better way. God wants you to face your fears and lean-in to who He desires you to be. If you're ready, Facing Your Fears is a great place to start.

Facing Your Fears, a 40-day, Scripture-driven devotional by Bethany Barr Phillips, helps reveal where fear has taken hold of your life and equips you to put an end to these strongholds.

TO VIEW SAMPLES OF FACING YOUR FEARS & TO ORDER, GO TO YM360.COM/FEARS

YOU HAVE AMAZING POTENTIAL TO IMPACT YOUR WORLD FOR CHRIST.

NOT TOMORROW. RIGHT NOW!

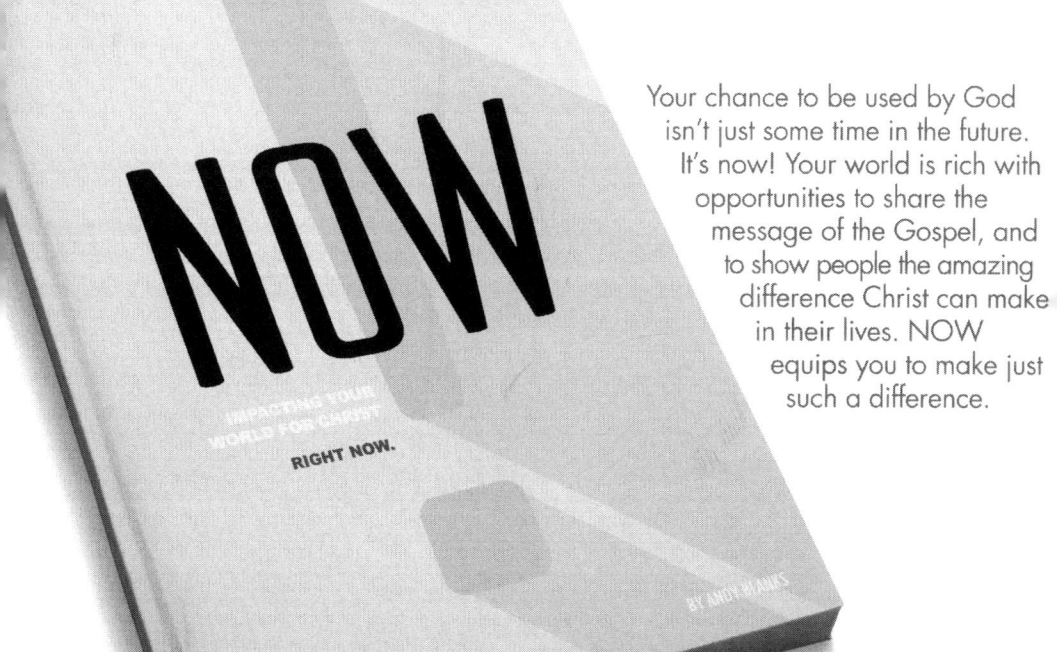

Your chance to be used by God isn't just some time in the future. It's now! Your world is rich with opportunities to share the message of the Gospel, and to show people the amazing difference Christ can make in their lives. NOW equips you to make just such a difference.

"NOW" WILL HELP YOU...
Understand the PURPOSE God has in store for you
Catch God's VISION for exactly how He wants to use you
PRACTICE real, practical ways to impact your world
Commit to ACTING on the opportunities God is giving you

TO VIEW SAMPLES OF NOW & TO ORDER, GO TO YM360.COM/NOW